THE COURAGE TO SUCCEED
A TRUE AMERICAN DREAM

ROSABEL V. ZOHFELD

ISBN: 979-8-89075-919-1

To order more copies, visit the author's website: www.rosabelunscripted.com

TABLE OF CONTENTS

DEDICATION

This book is dedicated to the memory of my mother, whose unwavering love and boundless wisdom continue to inspire me every day. Her spirit lives on in these pages, guiding my journey with her enduring grace and strength.

To my beloved children, may you always find courage and joy in every step of your path. Your laughter and curiosity are my greatest treasures, and my hope is that this book serves as a testament to the power of love and resilience that she instilled in us all.

To my wonderful husband, whose steadfast support and love provides the foundation upon which I build my dreams. Your partnership means the world to me.

And to those angels called friends, whose kindness, understanding, and companionship make life's journey brighter and more meaningful. Your presence in my life is a gift I cherish deeply.

FOREWORD

When I began writing this book, I found myself delving deeply into the many experiences and influences that have shaped both my personal life and professional path. This isn't merely a collection of stories; it reflects my journey, woven together from the threads of joy, struggle, and moments of profound realization. Every chapter draws from a lifetime of learning and growth, marked by the triumphs and challenges that have guided me forward.

Writing this book has been as enlightening as it has been challenging. It has served as a reminder of the power of perseverance, the necessity of self-reflection, and the transformative magic of shared stories. Through these pages, my hope is that you find comfort, inspiration, and perhaps a piece of your own experience reflected in mine, allowing us to connect through the universal threads of our human journeys.

In sharing my story, I intend to offer the lessons I've learned along the way. It is my goal to provide a perspective that resonates with you to offer reflections and tools that might aid you in your own path. This book is a walk through time and memory as I revisit the footsteps of my past to better understand the road that lies ahead.

Come with me as I explore the profound impact of beginnings—like the complexities of identity—and the ongoing search for meaning in a world shaped by both history and hope.

As I write, I strive to remain as objective and truthful as possible, understanding that every story carries a personal, subjective element. My intention is never to offend or disrespect anyone. For those who have known me since childhood, I hope they'll see this book as a heart laid bare, full of honesty and respect—without exaggeration or omission. My life has been molded by countless experiences, both my own and those of others. In this book, I aim to offer a breath of fresh air, fostering both learning and healing.

Thank you for joining me on this journey. Your understanding and companionship are invaluable to me. May this book serve as a beacon of hope, strength, and love—an enduring testament to the power of shared stories and the resilience of the human spirit.

Warm regards,

Rosabel Zohfeld

To Billie Jean

I could not have written this book without talking about Billie Jean. She was the kind of person whose beauty wasn't just something you could see—it was something you could feel, like a warm light surrounding you, filling every space she entered. It radiated out from her in waves of love, kindness, and an undeniable warmth that made you feel like you mattered the moment she smiled at you.

I first met Billie Jean in 2005. I had just made the move from Tampa, Florida, to Dothan, Alabama—a decision born from the desire to start fresh, to escape the weight of the past, and to find a place where I could belong. After searching for a church home, something drew me to the First Church of the Nazarene. I'm still not sure if it was chance, divine intervention, or a little bit of both, but walking through those doors that Sunday, I felt an instant sense of purpose.

I remember the moment I met Billie Jean as though it happened only yesterday. Billie Jean stood by the door, greeting each person with such genuine affection. When I walked in, she looked up from the conversation she was having, her eyes lighting up as if she had known me for years.

"Welcome," she said, her voice warm and inviting. "I'm Billie Jean. So glad you're here." And that was it. From that very first greeting, I felt an overwhelming sense of peace. I knew I had found something I didn't even know I was missing—someone who could fill the space left by a mother I had lost years before.

Billie Jean and I became inseparable after that. It wasn't just about church anymore; it was about life—life shared together. She welcomed me into her family's fold like I was one of her own children. I spent countless afternoons in her cozy home, the smell of roast chicken and fresh biscuits filling the air as she scurried around the kitchen, preparing meals that tasted like home itself. I can still hear her voice, full of laughter, as she shared stories of her childhood in Alabama, stories that always ended with her shaking her head and laughing at herself as if life had been one big, wonderful adventure.

Holiday dinners at Billie Jean's were an experience all their own. The table would be laden with food—turkey, mashed potatoes, green beans, and, of course, her famous deviled eggs. The laughter of family and friends would echo through the house, and I would sit at her table, feeling the warmth of not just the food but the love that surrounded it. Mr. Billie, her husband, would always give me a hug when I arrived, and his steady presence—quiet but solid—made me feel like I was exactly where I needed to be.

One particular Christmas, I remember sitting in her living room with Billie Jean. She had this habit of gently tapping her fingers on the arm of the chair when she was thinking. "Rosabel," she said, her voice low and sincere, "you are exactly where you need to be. Don't ever doubt that." At the time, I didn't fully understand what she meant, but now, looking back, I realize that those words were a gift—a promise that even in my moments of uncertainty, I would always find my way.

Billie Jean wasn't just a friend; she was a constant light in the darkest of times. There were many nights when I found myself at her door, worn out and unsure of my next step, and she would let me in without hesitation. Her house became my refuge—a safe space to rest my head, to heal, to find clarity. I never had to ask for help. Billie Jean saw what I needed before I even knew myself. Her door was always open, and her embrace always felt like home.

She was my cheerleader, my encourager. I remember one particularly hard day when everything felt impossible, and I was questioning my choices. She sat across from me, looking me in the eye, and said, "You're going to make it. I know you will. You're stronger than you think, Rosabel." Her belief in me was unwavering, even when I couldn't see it in myself. It was in those moments that I understood what true unconditional love meant—accepting someone for who they are, flaws and all, and still seeing their potential.

Billie Jean didn't just support me from the sidelines—she celebrated every victory as if it were her own. When I graduated, she threw me a party, meticulously planning every detail, from the food to the decorations. "You deserve this," she said, her eyes sparkling with pride. And when it came time for my wedding, Billie Jean was right there beside me, organizing my reception, making sure every moment was perfect, from the music to the cake and even the tiniest of details. I still have the hand-written notes she made for the event—her way of ensuring nothing was forgotten. To her, everything I did mattered, and she made sure I knew it.

Then, in the blink of an eye, Billie Jean was gone. She passed away quietly at the age of 85 after a brief illness. I remember the day I got the news. The world seemed to freeze for a moment. I had promised her I would visit soon, but life got in the way—my own distractions, the pull of time slipping away. And now, I regret it. If there's one thing I wish I could change, it would be to have spent more time with her in those final months.

But even in her absence, Billie Jean's legacy lives on. She showed me what it meant to love freely and without conditions, to be a light in someone else's life even in the hardest of times. I often find myself channeling her spirit when I encounter someone in need when I see an opportunity to be in that safe place, that comforting presence. Her lessons continue to shape who I am, guiding me through the ups and downs of life.

Billie Jean was a rare soul, one of those people who comes into your life and leaves an indelible mark. I believe she was an angel in human form, sent to remind us all of the power of kindness, the strength of unconditional love, and the beauty of showing up for others, no matter what. Writing about her here is not just a tribute—it's my way of thanking her for changing my life in ways I'm still uncovering.

Thank you, Billie Jean, for everything. For your love, your kindness, and your unwavering belief in me. You were the mother I didn't know I needed. You will always hold a piece of my heart, and your memory will live on in every act of kindness I pass on to others.

Chapter 1 – In the Beginning

"The journey of a thousand miles begins with one step, but understanding where we come from provides the map for the path we take."

— Unknown

The Start of a Journey

It was a Friday, November 5th, 1982, in the small town of Sincelejo-Sucre, Colombia. My mother, Rocio, was 34 weeks pregnant, expecting a routine prenatal checkup. The weather that day was warm, the kind of sticky heat that clings to your skin, typical for a November afternoon. She made her way to the clinic, unaware that her life—and mine—was about to change forever.

Dr. Blanco, the OBGYN, examined her with a level of concern that was uncharacteristic for a regular appointment. "Are you ready to have this baby? Let's do it now. Your blood pressure is dangerously high," he said, his voice steady but urgent.

My mother's heart raced. She had been expecting an ordinary checkup, not this bombshell. She never had a chance to process the words before they whisked her into an emergency C-section. That evening, at around 5 PM, I made my unexpected entrance into the world.

A Father's Joy and a Daughter's Fragility

While my mother faced the sterile, cold world of the operating room, my father, Manuel, was full of joy. He had always been one to express his emotions openly, and he wanted the world to know he was a proud father. Without hesitation, he brought mariachis to the hospital. The sweet, melodic strains of "Eres mi Niña Bonita" filled the room—a song dedicated to me, his new daughter. The serenade carried his joy, a gift that echoed his love.

But as the music played, my mother's eyes stayed focused on me, her tiny, fragile daughter placed in an incubator. I had arrived prematurely, and as I lay there, barely 34 weeks old, my mother's eyes welled with tears. Fear gripped her heart as she wondered if I would survive. Even my three-year-old cousin Diana, who came to visit, remarked on my long, skinny legs with innocent curiosity.

In that moment, my tiny, vulnerable form embodied both hope and fear—a combination my mother would carry for the rest of her life.

The Town That Shaped Me

As I grew older, Sincelejo-Sucre became more than just the place I lived; it became a part of me. The town was filled with vibrant music, the rhythm of salsa and vallenato filling the streets. The air carried the unmistakable smells of arepas and empanadas, freshly fried and mouthwatering. I learned to appreciate the beauty of simple things, the warmth of family, and the richness of our Colombian heritage.

My parents, Rocio and Manuel, made sure to instill in me a deep love for our roots. Spanish traditions, the importance of family, and a sense of community became the foundation upon which I built my identity. But as I grew older, I also began to sense the cracks in the foundation—the complexities of my mother's past that would shape my journey.

My name—Rosabel—was a mix of creativity and fate. It was my father's idea to name me after a French name, *Rosabelle*. He liked the sound of it but decided to give it a Spanish twist by dropping the

"-le," making it *Rosabel*. Ironically, I later discovered that Rosabel was an English name. To add another layer to my identity, my mother chose Virginia as my middle name, a blend of English and Spanish that, like me, existed between two worlds.

A Glimpse into My Mother's Heart

I want to tell you about the most wonderful woman I've ever met—my mother, Rocio. Her name, meaning "morning dawn," was a fitting description of her nature. Known as "la seño" (the teacher) by the people in our town, she devoted 34 years of her life to teaching elementary school. But beyond her work in the classroom, she was a talented dress designer known for creating exquisite garments that were the talk of the town.

Toward the end of her life, she pursued a master's degree in arts, a testament to her dedication to personal growth. Her love for education and her unyielding desire to improve herself left a lasting impression on me. My mother wasn't just a teacher or an artist—she was a force of nature.

But my mother's heart was even bigger than her talents. She loved deeply and without reservation, always giving of herself, even when she had nothing left to give.

I often watched her act selflessly, going without to help others. The people in our town would say, "She would take bread out of her mouth to give to someone in need." This wasn't just a figure of speech—it reflected her essence. Her kindness wasn't just an act; it was woven into every fiber of her being.

Yet, beneath this selflessness lay an unspoken sadness. My mother came from a broken family. Her own mother had married young, between the ages of 12 and 14, to a man in his 30s. Her marriage was arranged as a transaction, with her father giving her away in exchange for land and animals. My mother was one of 14 children—only 11 of whom survived.

Her story was one of hardship, and though she rarely spoke about it, I could see the scars in her eyes. They weren't just physical; they were emotional wounds that shaped her every decision. The dysfunction of her childhood shaped her beliefs, her relationships, and her sense of self.

I often saw my mother cry—tears that reflected a deep yearning for the love she never fully received. She had this quiet belief that love had to be earned, that giving was the way to be valued. She'd often give gifts, hoping to fill the void within herself, to create connections where none existed.

But her generosity, which stemmed from a deep need for acceptance, was often exploited. I watched people take advantage of her kindness, and it troubled me deeply. I could feel the injustice in those moments, and there were times I felt like I had to protect her, to be the adult when she couldn't be. Even as a young girl, I was forced to be fiercely protective. My mother's vulnerability became my battle, and I carried that responsibility with me.

Despite the pain my mother carried, she was undeniably beautiful—inside and out. Her artistry was unmatched. She could take the simplest materials and turn them into intricate works of art. People often marveled at her "lovely hands" in Spanish. They would call her "manos maravillosas," admiring the delicate, skilled work she did.

In the classroom, she had a natural ability to connect with her students. She inspired them, earning their respect and admiration. Her legacy as an educator was profound, and her work left a lasting impact on our community.

But my mother's beauty wasn't just about her physical appearance or her talent—it was about her soul. She radiated warmth and gentleness, and even though life had dealt her many hardships, she never lost faith in the goodness of others. Despite everything—her traumatic past, the betrayals she faced—she kept giving. She continued to love and believe in humanity, seeing the best in people, even when they had given her every reason to doubt them.

Even though my mother's life was tragically short, her legacy lives on in the hearts of those who knew her. She was a beacon of light in a world that often felt dark. She never allowed bitterness to consume her, and her kindness became her most enduring mark on the world.

As I look back on her life, I see a woman who was both broken and whole, who carried the weight of the world yet managed to shine brighter than anyone I've ever known. Rocio's story is one of immense strength, a testament to the resilience of the human spirit. Her life may have been filled with pain, but her love—her relentless, unwavering love—was a light that will never fade.

Her legacy is not just in the lessons she taught or the art she created—it is in the love she gave so freely, even when the world gave her little in return. And for that, she will never be forgotten.

CHAPTER 2 –CHILDHOOD

"Childhood is the most beautiful of all life's seasons, full of wonder, discovery, and the magic of growing up."

— ***Unknown***

The Dark Streets of Colombia

It was August 18, 1989. I was only six years old, but the image remains indelibly etched in my memory. The assassination of Luis Carlos Galán Sarmiento, a presidential candidate in Colombia, marked the beginning of the horrors my young mind would witness. In a country that had become a war zone during the Pablo Escobar era, it was hard to escape the constant danger. We didn't need a television to understand the violence; it was right there in the streets.

Walking with my mother through the central plaza, the air thick with the heat of the day, I couldn't avoid the graphic, uncensored headlines of violent crimes splashed across the front pages of newspapers. My tiny hands grasped her dress as I tried to look away from the images of bloodshed, but they clung to my mind like ghosts. As a child, I learned more about death just by walking through the market than most medical students would in a morgue. The sounds of sirens of gunshots became the soundtrack of my early years.

That same year, I was eagerly awaiting my first day of elementary school. I can still picture my bunny-shaped backpack, half electric blue and half white, with bunny ears and moving eyes. I waited for the private transport to take me to school, my heart thumping with excitement. A Dalmatian caught my attention as it sniffed a palm leaf in the middle of the road. It was such a peaceful moment, so normal until everything changed in an instant.

A blue Jeep sped by, and before I could react, it struck the dog with a sickening thud. The animal's body jerked before crumpling on the pavement, lifeless. What followed was a scream so primal, so full of anguish, that it rattled my bones. The dog's owner, a woman, cried out, her voice raw with pain. At that moment, I felt the world shift beneath my feet. The horror of what I'd seen blanketed my mind, and I can't recall much after that. The image of the dead dog has stayed with me, as has the feeling of helplessness. It was the first time I truly understood how fragile life is.

The Theft of My Childhood

That sense of vulnerability grew stronger as I experienced other events that year. My mother did everything she could to shield me, but it wasn't enough. The environment we lived in was suffocating, filled with shadows of danger and uncertainty. I remember the year before when our house was robbed. I was only four years old, barely old enough to comprehend the meaning of theft.

My parents had hired a housekeeper that day before heading to work. I had no idea she would steal everything from us. I can still remember the sound of her ironing clothes, a rhythmic, soothing noise—until I saw her emptying my mother's closet and filling boxes with our belongings. I was so small, so naive, asking her what she was doing as if I hadn't noticed the growing pile of items. She grabbed my hand and led me outside, locking the door behind us. I found myself sitting alone on the front porch in my underwear. How could she leave me there, so exposed, so alone? When my mother arrived and found me, she screamed. I didn't understand why she was so upset—until I saw the emptiness inside the house.

The police caught the housekeeper later, and I was brought to the station as a witness. But as a four-year-old, I was too young to understand the weight of my testimony. I had to point out the woman who had stolen everything, who could have taken me from my family. It's an experience that haunts me to this day. Where were the adults who were supposed to protect me?

A Fight to Protect My Mother

Around that same time, I witnessed my parents in a heated argument. The air between them was charged, thick with tension. My father's anger, which had been bubbling beneath the surface for so long, exploded. In a fit of rage, he grabbed what I believed to be a shoe and threw it, aiming it at my mother. Without thinking, I jumped between them, my small body trying to protect the woman I loved.

The next thing I knew, the shoe struck me, and I felt a sharp pain near my eye. Blood poured down my face as the world around me erupted into chaos. My mother screamed, and I cried in pain, but I felt like I was stuck in a fog. My father stood frozen, and my mother, unsure of what to do, grabbed me and ran to our neighbors for help. The neighbor tried to stop the bleeding with cotton balls, pressing them against my skin, but nothing worked. The blood wouldn't stop.

In my confusion and fear, I remember feeling weightless. It was as if the world had tilted, and I was in a strange dream. Someone suggested dunking me in water to stop the bleeding—so they did. I was submerged, the coolness of the water doing nothing to quell the panic rising in my chest. Every second felt like an eternity.

When my mother finally decided to take me to the hospital, she cradled me in her arms, and we boarded a public bus. The sight of me—covered in blood, a child in pain—was enough to freeze the other passengers. Their eyes followed us as if we were ghosts, their faces filled with shock, but no one said a word. I can still hear the hushed whispers as we rode to the hospital, the slow drip of blood staining my mother's clothes.

When we arrived at the hospital, I was rushed into the emergency room. The bright lights hurt my eyes, and the voices of doctors and nurses blurred into a background hum. I remember a doctor looming over me, dropping something into my eye that made everything go dark. When I finally woke up, I was standing in front of a mirror, my left eye covered in bandages. I had come so close to losing it.

The Stain of a Dysfunctional Family

By the time I was five, I understood that my family was not like other families. My parents separated when I was only four, and I remember every detail of that day—sitting in the living room, the papers spread out before my mother and father. I watched the notary's dress swirl around her legs as she signed her name, sealing the end of my parents' marriage.

Even at that age, I refused to accept that I was the product of a broken family. I promised myself I wouldn't repeat the mistakes of my father, who I saw drowning in alcohol and rage. I would never be like him, never succumb to the destructive habits that marred my family.

I hated the reckless lifestyle of northern Colombian men—the drinking, the violence. I loathed the way they treated women as if they were property. My father's violent outbursts had been frequent, and I became terrified of the chaos he would create. Furniture would fly across the room, and knives would be thrown. It was pure madness. I often found myself praying that I would survive.

My Father's Transformation

I never expected my father to change, but he did. Alcohol no longer had a hold on him, and by my high school graduation, he had stopped drinking entirely. Perhaps age and illness softened him, but I couldn't help but wonder—did he ever truly heal? His temper had been his legacy, one that I feared would haunt me forever. But by the time I was twelve, I stood up to him. I was tired of the abuse, tired of feeling small. The last time he raised his hand to me, I refused to let him. I had finally grown strong enough to protect myself.

My mother was also enduring her own battle against him, physically and emotionally. One night, I couldn't take it anymore. I gave her an ultimatum: either he left us, or I would. I was just 12 years of age. It was the last night my father ever spent under our roof. We lost everything when the housekeeper had stolen our belongings, including my mother's savings. We were forced to sell our home, and my mother bought a lot in a middle-class neighborhood where she dreamed of building a new life for us.

The Struggle for Stability

I often think back to that lot and the hardship it would bring my mother. If I had known how much it would cost her health and happiness, I wonder if I would have let her buy it. But that's a story for another time.

I was around nine years old when my father made the decision to leave his teaching job in a rural town. The town, notorious for its guerrilla and paramilitary activity, had grown increasingly dangerous, especially after the first "burro bomba" explosion in the country occurred there. The bomb, strapped to a donkey, I can't remember if there was a loss of human life, but I know they destroyed the small room where my father had been staying. At first, I wasn't sure if I was imagining things, but I was certain this was the first "burro bomba" in Colombia. To confirm, I googled it, and the result read: "The first 'burro bomba' attack in Colombia, carried out by the now-extinct FARC, took place in the town of Chalán, municipality of Ovejas, Sucre, on March 12, 1996." It was a moment that irrevocably altered him. His refusal to return to that job caused him to lose his position, but it also marked the beginning of his deeper depression.

A New Beginning in Bogotá

A few months later, after several years of struggling with his identity, my father moved to Bogotá to start over. He took up photography, something he had always been passionate about. It was in the capital that he began to find a semblance of peace. But even there, life had its challenges. One day, while photographing a beautiful building, my father was mistaken for a spy. The police detained him, suspecting him of planting a bomb. Thankfully, he was released when they realized his only crime was curiosity. That was just one of many events that shaped my father's journey.

The Resilience of a Child

Throughout my childhood, we moved frequently—about twice a year, on average. I was used to leaving behind homes, memories, and friends. But when I turned fourteen, we finally settled into one place for two whole years. It was a brief respite in the chaos of our lives.

During those years, I often found myself taking on adult responsibilities. I helped my mother manage her finances, picking up her paycheck and ensuring that it didn't get wasted on trivial things. I learned early that life required resilience, especially when it seemed like everything was falling apart.

The Resilience of Home

Despite the instability, there were moments of peace that anchored me. My paternal grandmother's house was one such haven. The traditional palm and bahareque house, built with the same materials that once constructed our family home, felt like a slice of paradise.

Visiting her often deeply connected me to my roots. Her backyard, filled with fruit trees like oranges, mangoes, and guanabanas, was a peaceful paradise where I found comfort in the tranquil atmosphere. The hammock, swaying in the breeze, became my sanctuary, and the soothing sounds of nature helped me forget the worries of the world. Though my grandmother's home no longer exists. This memory is one I still cherish, and I hope to recreate that serenity one day.

Even in the midst of all the hardship, Christmas was a time of joy. The celebration was a deep-rooted tradition in our family. The Novenas de Aguinaldo, the carols, the nativity scenes—each part of the celebration wrapped me in warmth, a contrast to the coldness of the world around me. Christmas Eve was especially magical, with families gathering for dinner and the Misa de Gallo marking the birth of Jesus. The vibrant energy of the streets, the parades, and the fireworks painted a picture of resilience and joy in a country that had suffered so much.

Though I often joke about the seemingly endless holidays in Colombia—like the Day of the Potato—these celebrations reminded me that even in the darkest times, there was always something to celebrate. Always a reason to find joy.

Reflection and Continuation

As I reflect on these early years, I see how deeply they shaped me. The chaos, the pain, the instability—it all left its mark. But so did the moments of peace, the love of family, and the resilience of the human spirit. Life is never just one thing: it's a mixture of light and dark, joy and sorrow. And perhaps that's what makes it all so meaningful.

Chapter 3 – The Escobar Era

"The evil that men do lives after them; the good is oft interred with their bones."

— *William Shakespeare, Julius Caesar*

Colombia in the 1980s was not just a country in turmoil; it was a battlefield where the power of one man blurred the lines between right and wrong. The name Pablo Escobar became a symbol of both unimaginable wealth and ruthless violence, a paradox of a man who built his empire on blood and yet cloaked himself in generosity. His infamy stretched far beyond Colombia's borders, casting a shadow so vast that even today, his reign remains one of the darkest chapters in our nation's history.

1982 the year I was born, that same year Escobar made his audacious entry into Colombian politics. It is an unsettling thought—entering the world at the very moment, my country was descending into one of its most violent eras. From the moment I was old enough to understand, fear was an unspoken part of daily life. We did not speak of it openly, but it was in the air, lingering like smoke after an explosion. Even as a child, I understood that something was deeply wrong, even if I couldn't yet grasp the full extent of it.

The Rise of a Kingpin

Escobar's rise had begun in the 1970s, but by the time I was born, he had become more than just a drug lord—he was a force that dictated the pulse of the nation. Through the Medellín Cartel, he had built a global cocaine empire, flooding the United States with his product and amassing wealth beyond comprehension. He controlled politicians, police forces, and even the media. His power extended so deeply that his presence could be felt in the most mundane aspects of life—what news we were allowed to hear, which streets were safe to walk on, and which were suddenly stained with blood.

Then came his boldest move yet—his foray into politics. In 1982, Escobar was elected to the Colombian Congress as an alternate representative. To many, it was an unspeakable betrayal. A man who had built his fortune through murder and corruption now stood in a position of legislative power. He presented himself as a benefactor of the poor, funding housing projects, building soccer fields, and providing for the impoverished in ways the government never had. For some, he was a savior. For others, he was a wolf in sheep's clothing.

I often wonder how people justified supporting him. Was it fear? Was it necessity? Or was it simply the need to believe in something, even if that something was a lie? I was too young then to understand the complexities of human loyalty, but as I grew older, I began to see how desperation can turn criminals into heroes.

By the mid-1980s, Escobar's empire was at its peak. He was no longer just a criminal; he was a warlord ruling over a country gripped by terror. His infamous policy—*plata o plomo* (silver or lead)—left no room for negotiation. Bribery or bullets. Wealth or death. Those who dared to stand against him found themselves silenced, their deaths serving as messages to anyone who might challenge his rule.

The Colombian government attempted to confront him, but corruption ran too deep. In 1984, when I was just two years old, Escobar struck a deal that allowed him to serve his sentence in *La Catedral*. This prison was more of a fortress, built to his specifications, complete with a soccer field, a jacuzzi, and luxuries beyond imagination. The world mocked the Colombian government, calling it a farce. But inside the country, there was no laughter, only the grim realization that justice had become just another casualty of Escobar's war.

Even in captivity, he ruled. Orders were given. Murders were arranged. The drug trade continued. When authorities finally attempted to transfer him to a real prison in 1992, Escobar simply walked out. His escape unleashed a new wave of terror, one that would define my childhood.

It is difficult to explain what it is like to grow up in a war you cannot see yet feel in every aspect of your existence. The streets of Bogotá and Medellín were never truly silent, but there was a stillness—a collective inhalation of breath before another explosion, another assassination. By the time I was old enough to truly understand, I had already learned that safety was an illusion.

One of the defining moments of my childhood was the 1989 bombing of Avianca Flight 203, orchestrated by Escobar to kill a presidential candidate. Instead, it killed over a hundred innocent people. I was too young to fully grasp the magnitude of the event, but I remember my parents' faces when they heard and watched the news. I remember my mother clutching the edge of the kitchen table, whispering prayers under her breath. I remember my father's quiet rage, his knuckles white against the table as the details were broadcasted.

And then there was the assassination of Luis Carlos Galán, a presidential candidate who had dared to stand against Escobar. He was killed in 1989, shot in front of a crowd. I was seven years old, but I remember the image of his lifeless body on the news, the way the adults in the room stiffened, and how the silence stretched out for too long. Even then, I knew we had lost something important.

Public spaces became war zones. Shopping malls, political rallies, newspaper offices—no place was safe. We learned to live cautiously, avoid crowds, always alert to the possibility that the wrong place at the wrong time could mean death.

The Fall of a Tyrant

By 1992, Escobar was on the run. His former allies turned against him. The Colombian government, with U.S. support, intensified efforts to bring him down. He was no longer untouchable. The man who had once ruled Colombia with absolute impunity was now a fugitive. But no empire lasts forever.

On December 2, 1993, it ended. Escobar was found and killed on a rooftop in Medellín. The news spread quickly, and I remember that day with absolute clarity. I was 11 years old. People poured into the streets. Some celebrated, others mourned. The contradictions of his life were reflected in his death.

I remember feeling an odd sense of emptiness. The fear that had shaped my childhood was suddenly—almost unnervingly—gone. But what would replace it? The damage had already been done. The wounds he inflicted on Colombia were not just physical; they were psychological and emotional. An entire generation had grown up in his shadow, and the scars of his reign would take decades to heal.

The Escobar era left deep scars in Colombia. It was a time when one man's ambition dictated the fate of an entire nation. Yet, in the face of chaos, there was resilience. There were those who fought back, those who survived, and those who rebuilt.

I think about the people who lost their lives, the families who were torn apart, the children—like me—who had to grow up too fast. But I also think about the strength of my country, about how we refused to be defined by our darkest years.

Escobar's legacy is one of devastation, but it is also a lesson—a warning against unchecked power, a testament to the fragility of justice. But more importantly, it is a reminder that even in the darkest of times, there is resistance. There is hope.

And hope, no matter how fragile, is what allows nations to rise again.

CHAPTER 4 – MY FATHER'S JOURNEY

"The greatest legacy one can pass on to one's children and grandchildren is not money or other material things accumulated in one's life, but rather a legacy of character and faith."

– Rev. Billy Graham.

Early Life and Catholic Roots

I vividly remember the shift in my father's life when I was around five years old. It was 1987, and it would be the last time I saw him drunk on the porch of our home. At the time, I couldn't fully comprehend what was happening, but something inside him changed not long after. The man I had known—flawed, struggling, yet loving—underwent a transformation so profound that it altered the course of not only his life but mine as well.

My father was born in Corozal, Sucre, Colombia, steeped in Roman Catholic tradition. As a young boy, he served as an altar server, absorbing Catholic teachings and traditions. His faith was ingrained in his identity, yet it remained more of a cultural practice than a personal conviction. His early education at the Escuela Normal in Corozal set him on the path to becoming an educator, and he spent years teaching in schools across the Sucre Department.

On the surface, his life seemed stable, structured by his work, family, and faith. However, beneath that, he carried burdens he didn't openly share. Social drinking was commonplace in his environment, but for him, it became an escape, a way to cope with disappointments and pressures. My mother, a devout Catholic who had once considered becoming a nun, watched in silent concern, but it wasn't until fate intervened that my father's life took a drastic turn.

The Turning Point

Assigned to a teaching position in Chalán, Sucre, a small rural town, my father found himself facing unexpected hardship. One day, he fell gravely ill, his condition worsening despite medical attention and traditional remedies. No doctor could pinpoint the cause, and as his health deteriorated, he reached a point of desperation.

It was then that Arnold, the brother of a little girl named Milka, who was my dad's first-grade student, suggested he visit her family's evangelical church, where they often prayed for healing. My father was not a man to easily embrace change, especially one that veered so far from his Catholic upbringing. But with nowhere else to turn, he went.

At that church, the congregation gathered around him in fervent prayer, and the pastors laid hands on him. He later described an overwhelming sensation of warmth and light washing over him, an inexplicable release from his suffering. That day, he walked out not only physically healed but spiritually awakened. He would later tell me that he believed he had been under a witchcraft spell—a belief not uncommon in some regions of Colombia.

Struggles and Growth

My father's healing was undeniable, but what followed was an even greater transformation. Almost immediately, he quit smoking and drinking—habits that had long been a part of his life. Yet, his spiritual rebirth did not come without its struggles. He wrestled with doubt, questioning whether this newfound faith could truly anchor him through life's difficulties.

He also grappled with the implications of his conversion. Could he turn away from the traditions he had known since childhood? Catholicism was not just a religion; it was an identity, a familial and cultural connection that had shaped his entire upbringing. The idea of worshiping God directly, without intermediaries like priests or saints, felt almost like a betrayal. But as he immersed himself in the Bible, he found answers that solidified his new convictions.

He embraced three fundamental beliefs:

1. There is only one mediator between God and humanity—Jesus Christ (1 Timothy 2:5).
2. Salvation comes through no other name but Jesus (Acts 4:12).
3. Jesus is the way, the truth, and the life, and no one can come to the Father except through Him (John 14:6).

Despite his conversion, my father never abandoned his respect for the Virgin Mary as the mother of his saviour Jesus Christ. He taught me that while they were to be honored, worship belonged to God alone. His journey was not one of rejection but of redirection, shifting from religious ritual to personal faith.

As my father embraced his calling into evangelical and missionary work, my mother remained devoted to Catholicism. Raised in a strict Catholic household, she held firm to the practices she had known since childhood. Naturally, I was brought up in a Catholic environment, attending a school where we prayed the rosary daily, honored the Virgin Mary, and celebrated Catholic traditions.

Yet, at home, my father's teachings instilled in me a different perspective. He emphasized the importance of a direct relationship with God, one that did not require intermediaries. I found myself torn between these two worlds—participating in school prayers while silently directing my heart to God in my own way.

This internal conflict was not one of rebellion but of searching. Even as a child, I felt a strong conviction that my connection with God was deeply personal, shaped not by routine but by a genuine relationship. My father's faith was not forced upon me; rather, his testimony served as a living example of transformation and grace.

One of my earliest memories of witnessing my father's devotion was the first time he took me to an evangelical church. The contrast was stark. Unlike the solemn rituals of Catholic masses, this congregation sang with passion, raised their hands in worship, and prayed with a sense of urgency. I was captivated by the sincerity of their faith, the raw emotion that filled the room. It was unlike anything I had ever experienced.

Over time, my own faith journey began to take shape. I saw how my father's belief gave him strength, purpose, and peace. Watching him overcome his struggles and dedicate his life to God inspired me to develop my personal relationship with Jesus Christ. His testimony was no longer just his—it became the foundation upon which my own faith was built.

Looking back, I see how my father's spiritual awakening not only changed him but also set the course for my life. His devotion to God taught me resilience, faith, and the power of grace. His story was not just about finding religion; it was about transformation, about the courage to step into the unknown and embrace a calling beyond his own understanding.

I am deeply grateful for my father's guidance and the foundation he laid for me in faith and education. His unwavering devotion to God helped me forge my own path, one that continues to define who I am today. This relationship with God has been my anchor, guiding me through life's challenges, shaping my values, and influencing the way I live and interact with the world.

His journey reminds me that faith is not about perfection but about persistence, about choosing to trust even when the road ahead is unclear. That is the legacy he left me—a legacy I strive to pass on, not just through words, but through the life I live every day.

CHAPTER 5 – THE BETRAYAL

"Crocodiles are easy. They try to kill and eat you. People are harder. Sometimes, they pretend to be your friend first."

— Steve Irwin

The Wound of Betrayal

Betrayal is not simply an injury; it's a jagged tear in the fabric of your world, a wound that runs so deep it changes you forever. The pain doesn't just reside in the heart; it seeps into your soul, leaving scars that never quite heal. When it comes from those you trust—those you've laughed with, cried with, and shared your most intimate thoughts with—it's an agony that cuts deeper than any external wound. My mother, a woman whose life was defined by kindness and trust, had always believed in the goodness of others. She never expected the sharp sting of betrayal, least of all from those she called friends.

I still can't place the exact date, but I remember the day with a clarity that makes it feel as if it happened just yesterday. I was 15, walking home from school with the rhythm of my footsteps familiar and comforting. But the moment I opened the door, something in the air shifted. A stillness. A heaviness. It was like the world was holding its breath. I stepped inside and found my mother lying on her bed. Her face, usually vibrant and full of life, was ghostly pale. Her eyes were wide, filled with fear, the kind of fear I had never seen in her before.

She didn't move when I walked in; she just stared at me. Her usual warmth was absent, replaced by an emptiness I couldn't understand. She looked smaller somehow, vulnerable, as though she had been stripped of her strength.

I stood frozen, unsure of what to do or say. The silence between us felt suffocating, a sharp contrast to the usual comfort we shared. A neighbor who had accompanied her to the hospital finally spoke, his voice shaking as he recounted the morning's events. My mother had gone to the bank to withdraw a significant amount of her retirement savings, the fruits of decades of hard work. She had planned to secure our future, a simple act with good intentions. But as she crossed the empty parking lot after leaving the bank, a man had emerged, his face hidden beneath the shadow of a baseball cap, a gun pressed to her side.

"Give me the bag," he had demanded, his voice cold, devoid of any human warmth.

Her fingers had tightened around the bag, her mind racing for a way to keep it safe. The pain in her arm came so suddenly, so sharply, that she felt it before she even had time to scream. Darkness swallowed her up, her body collapsing like a ragdoll. When she finally woke up, disoriented and terrified, the only thing she could remember was a blank, gaping void where everything else should have been. Somehow, she had found her way to the neighbor's house, but the bag was gone. And in its place? A cruel joke—stacks of newspapers wrapped to look like cash.

The doctors later confirmed what we feared. My mother had been drugged with scopolamine, a substance that, when administered, could erase the victim's memory, leaving them with nothing but fragmented, distorted recollections of the event.

A Mockery of Trust

But the robbery wasn't the only theft. The money, the symbol of my mother's sacrifice, was gone—but worse was the realization that the trust she had extended to those around her had been shattered. What followed sent a shiver down my spine. During the police investigation, it came to light that the robbers had been tipped off—

by someone inside the bank. But as the details of the crime began to unravel, the true horror emerged. The police suspected that two of my mother's closest friends might have been involved.

The day before the robbery, she had casually mentioned to them, over coffee, that she planned to withdraw fifteen million pesos—the exact amount the robbers had stolen—a seemingly innocent conversation shared in the safety of a long-standing friendship. Yet, as the timing of the crime unfolded, a sickening realization set in: the very people my mother had trusted most were now suspected of being involved in her betrayal.

A Pattern of Deceit

This wasn't the first time my mother had been betrayed by someone she held close. Years earlier, when she sold our family home to buy land in an upscale neighborhood, she believed she was investing in our future. But then, a friend persuaded her to sell that land and invest the proceeds into their family business, promising steady returns. It seemed like a golden opportunity. My mother, ever trusting, agreed.

But as time wore on, the investment crumbled. Financial pressures mounted. When my mother tried to reclaim her investment, she was met with cold indifference. The friend denied ever owing her anything. "You took the money as merchandise," she claimed, her words cutting like a knife.

The betrayal was more than just financial. It was personal. It was a betrayal of trust. My mother was devastated, not just by the loss of money but by the loss of something more sacred—the belief that people could be relied upon. The friend, who had once been like family, now stood as a figure of indifference. My mother, her spirit broken, boarded a bus that day—and she never returned.

At her funeral, the absence of this so-called friend was a silent accusation. Her husband offered weak excuses, but those words only solidified the betrayal. And in that moment, I understood betrayal isn't just about the act; it's about the aftermath—the people who turn their backs, the ones who remain silent when they should speak. Betrayal has a way of spreading like a virus, infecting everything and everyone it touches.

Even years later, the wounds remain. The bitterness of those betrayals has been hard to shake. But instead of letting the bitterness take root in my heart, I've chosen a different path. I've let go of the anger, releasing it like a weight that's too heavy to carry. I've placed my faith in something greater, trusting that, in the end, justice will prevail and the truth will come to light. I know the pain of losing my mother will never fully fade. But I also know that, in time, the truth will emerge, and the lies will be exposed for what they are.

The lessons of those betrayals are not lost on me. They have taught me that trust is fragile, a delicate thing that requires care and protection. Yet, despite the pain they caused, I refuse to let those betrayals define me. Instead, I choose to honor the lessons they've imparted. I've learned to cherish the trust I share with others, to hold it sacred, and to never let the bitterness of the past cloud my ability to believe in the goodness of people.

My mother's ability to continue trusting, even after all she endured, remains one of the most powerful lessons I carry with me. She taught me that resilience isn't about hardening your heart or becoming cynical. It's about keeping your heart open, even when the world feels like it's conspiring against you. It's about holding on to hope, even when everything around you seems bleak. And above all, it's about the courage to keep believing in the goodness of people, no matter how many times that belief is shaken.

Through it all, I've come to realize that trust is not a given. It's a fragile gift that must be earned, protected, and respected. The people we allow into our lives, the ones we love and cherish, are capable of both kindness and cruelty. My mother's ability to trust, even after being betrayed so many times, is both heartbreaking and inspiring. Her faith in others was never blind; it was simply a reflection of the kindness and generosity she carried in her heart.

But the truth is, trust is not easily given. It is earned with time, with consistency, and with actions that reflect our values. And while betrayal will always sting, it does not have to define us. The scars may remain, but they do not dictate our future. My mother's life was marred by betrayal, but it was also filled with love, with kindness, and with resilience. And that is the legacy she left behind.

CHAPTER 6 – CURVEBALLS

"Adversity introduces a man to himself."

— Albert Einstein.

Life had always felt like a carefully plotted map. I followed its paths to school, routines, and goals. There was certainty. But all that certainty vanished the day my mother died. What I couldn't know then was that the curveballs I'd face in the coming months would challenge everything I thought I knew about myself. Let me take you back to a moment before it all fell apart—a moment of pure joy.

November 20, 1999. My high school graduation. The air was thick with celebration, a pride so intense I could almost taste it. It felt like a victory lap, like the first step into a new world that was open and waiting for me. That was supposed to be the last memory I carried with me from that time. A promise of a bright future. But in the blink of an eye, the world as I knew it would collapse.

The Presence of Loss

The morning of Saturday, December 11, 1999. The world shifted.

I woke up, confusion clouding my thoughts. My head felt heavy, my limbs stiff. The room was too quiet, and the disorientation took over, making the bed feel unfamiliar beneath me. I was lying on my back, but I had no recollection of how I got there. Something was wrong—something was off—but it didn't seem real enough to be worried about.

Mireya's voice broke through the haze. "Your mother left early for errands, but she left money for lunch."

My stomach churned. *My mother left without a word.* She always tended to make sure everyone knew when she was going somewhere, especially on a Saturday morning. Something didn't sit right, but I pushed it aside. There was no time to focus on the strange feeling in my chest.

I glanced at the clock: 11 a.m. I blinked, confused. I never slept that late. The time seemed to be suspended in place. I looked down at myself, feeling like a stranger in my own skin. My body didn't respond the way it usually did. I tried to shake it off. *I'm just tired. I just need more sleep.*

Confusion and Rumors

Finally, after much pondering, I dragged myself to the dinning table to eat. The minutes stretched, each one hanging in the air like a weighted blanket. I stared at the clock again—12:30. Then, the seconds began to crawl slower than I had ever felt them. It was as though time itself was mocking me, reminding me how completely out of control I was.

At 12:35, something happened. It was subtle, barely noticeable, but it sent a ripple through the air—a presence moving down the hallway. I caught a glimpse of something—someone—a figure, no, something more ethereal, drifting in front of me. It stopped. Just for a moment, right beside me. I felt it, the lightest pressure on my cheek, like a kiss. I froze; my breath caught in my throat. A flash of my mother's face, pale and lifeless, flashed in my mind—a casket. My chest tightened.

I shook my head. *No. This couldn't be real.* But it wasn't going away. I stood up, feeling restless and afraid, my thoughts spinning. I stumbled to the neighbor's house, my legs weak beneath me. The air around me felt thicker with every step, the sense of impending doom following me like a shadow.

Minutes later, my cousin arrived, her face ashen. Without a word, she pulled me close. "They think it's a heart attack," she said softly, each word dripping with disbelief. The weight of it pressed on my chest.

My feet moved automatically, though I didn't remember deciding to walk. We went to her house, only a few blocks away, but each step felt like miles as if the ground beneath me was sinking with every movement. When we reached the house, I didn't need anyone to say it. My aunt walked in, her eyes vacant, not a word spoken. I looked at her face and knew. My world split in two.

"No… no…" I whispered, barely able to breathe through the tightness in my throat. I felt a heavy weight settle on my heart like it was being crushed. But then, somewhere deep inside me, a strange hardness rose. I didn't understand it, but I accepted it. "Let me change. I'll go wherever," I said, my voice shaking but determined to keep going.

But the others didn't understand. They looked at me with pity as if I were a broken thing. I wasn't broken; I was just… moving forward, trying to. The grief would catch up to me soon enough, but for now, I had to keep going. My feet had to move.

Later, I would learn that my mother had passed at 12:35 p.m.—the exact moment I felt her presence. I stood over her casket, numb, my mind whirling. I longed to speak with her one last time. To ask for forgiveness, for understanding. To beg for peace, but it was not meant to be.

Instead, what I found were whispers. Accusations. People were speaking behind my back, their voices thick with the weight of speculation. "She must've done it herself," someone muttered. The rumor was suicide. They said she had ingested formaldehyde, that she'd been found in an odd place, far from home. None of it made sense. The words floated around me like smoke, but I couldn't breathe in the fog of confusion.

Someone told me my mother had collapsed at a stranger's door, foaming at the mouth. I couldn't make sense of the chaos, the conflicting stories. I wanted answers, but the more I searched, the more the rumors grew. Each new claim made the pain deeper. People looked at me with accusatory eyes as if my grief was somehow a sign of guilt.

I knew I had to leave to escape from the rumors and the relentless whispers. I was brought to a counselor, a woman who had never truly known me, in the hopes that she could help me and guide me through the grief, but instead, she shocked me with a prediction that felt cold and dismissive: "You may follow your mother."

The words echoed in my mind, jarring and insensitive. How could she assume so much about me and reduce my entire life to a statistic? Her words dismissed my individuality, my autonomy. It was as though she didn't believe I could carve my own path. But I refused to accept that. I refused to let anyone—especially her—dictate my life. The stubbornness I carried wasn't a curse. It was the very thing that kept me fighting, kept me moving when the world tried to drown me.

After my mother's death, I stayed with her older sister for four months. There were moments of gratitude but also discomfort. I couldn't ignore the way my aunt kept records of every expense. When the life insurance money came, my aunt handed me a bill. A bill for everything she'd spent on me—each purchase written down in her meticulous notebook. She didn't add the cost of food, but she was willing to charge my father for that later.

It stung deeper than I wanted to admit. The love I had been given felt somehow tainted by the transactional nature of family. But I paid for it. I had no choice. The relationship had shifted in ways I wasn't ready for, but I had learned early to swallow my pride and keep moving forward.

Later, when I moved in with my grandmother, another shift occurred. The demands were more direct. "You need to contribute to groceries," my mom's younger sister demanded, placing a bill before me. 300,000 Colombian pesos a month. They assumed my mother's pension would cover it, but that pension was a meager 600.000 pesos a month, an equivalent amount of $250 today.

During this time, Jaime—a lawyer and trusted friend—became a guiding force. He saw my struggle and helped me navigate one of the hardest decisions I had to make: transferring my mother's pension to my father.

Years later, I would learn that my mother had saved my grandmother's house from foreclosure. She'd sacrificed her own dreams to keep the roof over our heads. The irony was sharp when I was asked to sign the papers transferring ownership to my mom's youngest sister. The small amount of money I received barely covered my airfare to Colombia. I was left with nothing but the bitter taste of sacrifice, of things I never knew until it was too late.

CHAPTER 7 – CAREER FORMING

"The only limit to our realization of tomorrow will be our doubts of today."

– *Franklin D. Roosevelt*

A Dream of Medicine

I was five years old when I decided, in my young mind, that I would become a physician. The thought lodged itself in my heart, not as a mere fantasy, but as something real. By the time I graduated high school in 1999, that childhood dream felt like a promise to myself. It was something I held onto tightly, even as the reality of life began to strip away the simple optimism of my youth.

In 2000, I enrolled at "La Universidad de Sucre" to study biology, but something didn't feel right. The lecture halls, filled with students full of ambition, seemed distant to me as if I was only observing from the outside. I soon faced a new reality: after a semester, I had to move to Barranquilla, a bustling coastal city in northern Colombia. The sound of the ocean echoed in my ears as I settled into my grandmother's home, her heavy sighs making it clear she wasn't pleased with my decision.

I fought for a spot at the medical school there, but every door I knocked on stayed closed. The private institution demanded fees I couldn't afford. With no family to co-sign a loan, I stood at the threshold, watching others walk through doors I couldn't enter. The only option was to wait for the following year. The waiting felt like a slow, gnawing hunger. Still, I had everything but the financial support to make this dream a reality.

A Dream Deferred

It wasn't long before the weight of my situation became unbearable. My grandmother's cold words dug into me, blaming me for the death of my mother. It felt like a fog descended over everything I thought I knew. In class, surrounded by my peers, I sat with tears threatening to spill over. I could no longer hold it in. The walls felt too tight, and I knew I needed to leave. I couldn't continue to afford medical school.

I left without a plan, wandering aimlessly until a quiet street led me to a martial arts school. The hum of movement, the rhythm of punches and kicks in the air, drew me in like a magnet. I approached the manager, my voice tight with vulnerability. I told him my story. He nodded thoughtfully and then offered me a small room to live in at the school, with only one condition: work toward earning a black belt. He said it would take a year if I practiced every day.

I didn't hesitate. "A year," I whispered to myself. And with that, the course of my life shifted. Each drop of sweat in the dojo, each aching muscle, fueled me. I moved in, feeling the rough texture of the tatami mats beneath my feet as I began my daily rituals.

The Black Belt Challenge

The first few months were grueling. The scent of sweat and worn leather filled the air as I threw punch after punch, kick after kick. My body felt foreign to me—clumsy, stiff, unsure. But every evening, I returned to the dojo, sometimes feeling like I was dragging my feet across the floor but still pushing forward.

As the year drew to a close, I registered for the black belt conference in a distant city. My mind buzzed with anticipation, my heart a rhythm of hope. Yet, when I stood before the instructor, ready to show him the result of my dedication, he refused. He offered an excuse: another female student, according to him, was more prepared but lacked the financial means. The moment he said it, I felt the rush of heat fill my chest. It wasn't fair. It wasn't right.

But I knew my worth. I was ready. The words of my instructor felt like a weight pressing down on me, trying to make me doubt myself. But instead, I stood taller. With permission from the primary master, I went ahead. I was met with anger from my instructor, whose hands clenched into fists. "If you go, you'll never return here," he threatened. The challenge was clear. I didn't back down.

I left for the black belt conference with a fire in my chest. When I returned, my body ached with exhaustion, but my heart swelled with pride. I had earned my black belt in Shaolin Fa-Men-Chuan (Kung-Fu), something I had worked toward tirelessly. But still, my focus began to shift. My education called me back.

It was during this time that I met Ana Lucia, a fellow student who noticed the quiet struggle behind my eyes. Every morning, she appeared at the dojo with a fruit juice in hand, rich in protein, knowing that food had become a luxury I could barely afford. Her kindness was a flicker of warmth in the coldness of my world.

Ana Lucia's parents invited me to stay with them, a gesture that felt like a lifeline. I didn't think twice. I packed my meager belongings and moved in. Their cozy home radiated warmth and generosity. I didn't have to ask for help—it was simply offered, a quiet blessing I hadn't anticipated.

A New Land, A New Start

The opportunity to immigrate to the United States was a dream come true, yet it wasn't without its own set of hurdles. I landed in this new world on April 4, 2004—my freedom, my new beginning. The air felt different, and the ground beneath my feet seemed to offer a fresh start. I wanted to kiss it. I felt like a bird released from a cage, wings stretched wide.

The process of becoming a legal resident was slow, tedious, and at times overwhelming. But I didn't wait idly. I got behind the wheel of a car for the first time. The steering wheel was unfamiliar to my hands, but my mind was clear and focused. How difficult could it be, I thought? The journey was long, but every step brought me closer to my goal.

I enrolled in my first college classes. It wasn't easy. I started from the basics—English 000, Math 000—but there was a spark inside me, a fire that kept me going. I wasn't just studying to get through it. I was building something from the ground up. I had to work during the day and go to school at night to support myself.

The Nursing Journey

By February 2009, I decided to join the Air Force. It seemed like the perfect opportunity: a path to citizenship, a chance to serve my new country, and a way to gain experience in the medical field. But the military, as much as I tried, felt out of reach. I wasn't a citizen yet, and without that, my aspirations to serve as a medic were dashed.

Instead, I focused on something else. I enrolled in EMT classes that fall, throwing myself into the coursework with the same intensity I had brought to martial arts. I finished the course by the end of 2009 and began taking pre-nursing sciences in 2010, eventually earning an associate degree in science.

In 2011, I received my acceptance letter from Troy University's nursing school. I felt my heart race with excitement, my breath shallow. The dream that had started as a young girl in Colombia was now within reach.

As nursing school progressed, I found myself working harder than ever. Juggling multiple jobs, including working at a high school cafeteria and teaching Spanish to children, I stretched myself thin to make ends meet. My hands often smelled of bread and cheese from making sandwiches, or my fingers were stained from textbooks and lesson plans.

But the kindness of others never ceased to surprise me. One family from Puerto Rico took me in, giving me a home for months. Later, a neighboring Army officer preparing for deployment offered me a place to stay rent-free. He entrusted me with his properties, and I cared for them as if they were my own. These acts of generosity were not expected but deeply appreciated. I felt like I had been sent angels when I needed them most.

When the time came, I accepted student loans to cover living costs. It wasn't easy, but it was a step toward my future. After a couple of years of financial struggle, I finally secured my own apartment.

The Road Ahead

Looking back, I see that every step, no matter how painful, led me here. I graduated from nursing school and began my career in the emergency room of a hospital in Alabama. It was a tough job, serving a community with limited resources, where patients waited for hours just to be seen.

But I didn't focus on the long hours or the pain in my feet from standing all day. Instead, I focused on my patients. I didn't look at their backgrounds, skin color, or accents. I saw them for who they truly were: human beings in need of care.

Now, as a nurse practitioner, I carry with me the lessons of resilience, generosity, and hard work. My path was never easy, but each challenge shaped me. I don't just care for people as a professional; I care for them because I see the Creator in each person. And this belief continues to guide me as I walk forward on this incredible journey.

Chapter 8 – Belonging, Not Fitting

"My consciousness of belonging to the invisible community of those who strive for truth, beauty, and justice has preserved me from feeling isolated."

— Albert Einstein.

Between Two Worlds: A Struggle for Belonging

For much of my journey, I've lived in the space between belonging and fitting in, a limbo where neither world fully accepted me. It was a kind of emotional tug-of-war. When I first arrived in the United States, I couldn't shake the feeling that I didn't quite belong here, yet I also no longer felt at home in Colombia.

There were moments when the weight of this dissonance hit me hard. I remember, at times, staring at the wall, feeling like a ghost between two places. I wasn't a part of the culture I had come from, nor could I yet be a part of the one I was trying to build. The blend of my Colombian heritage and my new life was a constant push and pull, a quiet ache of wanting to be both and yet not fully belonging to either.

But over the years, I've found that being in limbo isn't as terrible as it sounds. It's been a space of discovery. Slowly, I've come to realize that the struggle to find belonging has been crucial to understanding who I truly am. Through the tension of this in-between place, I've learned to speak out, challenge norms, and stand firm in my identity. Speaking against injustice, standing up for the voiceless, and questioning the status quo have all become an essential part of who I am.

One of the first things that threw me into the deep end of cultural misunderstanding was the constant questioning of my identity. I had no idea how many people would confuse my Colombian roots with other places or people. The first time it happened, I was caught off guard.

It was a typical day at the front desk, where I worked as a receptionist. A man came in, and when I asked for his last name, he replied with an answer I wasn't prepared for. "English," he said. I blinked, not sure if I had misunderstood. "Sir, your last name?" I repeated. He stared at me, slightly annoyed. "English." I finally asked, "Am I speaking French to you or what?" He let out a laugh and responded, "No, my last name is English!"

It was an awkward and unexpected moment of humor, but I laughed along with him, even though I wasn't sure whether to be embarrassed or amused. At that moment, I realized that humor had become my shield—my way of diffusing the constant misunderstandings that seemed to follow me.

Other moments weren't as funny. I was paying at a cashier when a woman looked at my olive skin and asked where I was from. "Colombia," I replied proudly, but the confusion that followed was anything but humorous. She tilted her head and said, "Oh, South Carolina?" Before I could respond, another woman in line joined in, "Girl, don't you know where Columbia is? It's that country next to Cuba, right?" I could feel my cheeks flush. I wanted to correct them, to explain how much of a difference there is between Colombia and South Carolina, but instead, I smiled and responded, "Surely it is."

These moments, though frustrating, became opportunities for cultural exchange. I took to responding to the question "Where are you from?" with a bit of humor. "Do you really want to know?" I would say. "Okay, I'm from the deep-deep south." The inevitable response was usually always, "South Carolina?" And I would grin, "Nope, South America." The laughter that followed always felt like a small victory—a way to educate and challenge misconceptions with kindness.

However, not every encounter was lighthearted. I will never forget the day I was called into my boss's office. Apparently, someone had complained about me talking too much about Colombia and smiling too much. My supervisor's disdain for me was palpable. "If you're so proud to be Colombian, why are you here?" she asked with a sneer. "Why are you always smiling?" The remark about the mail not arriving on a donkey was an insult wrapped in a joke, one that stung more than I cared to admit.

Her words haunted me. My smile, something so inherently part of my nature, was a source of mockery. For a moment, I wondered if I should change. Maybe I should stop smiling so much. Maybe I should stop talking about my culture. But deep down, I knew that altering myself to fit their expectations wasn't the answer. My identity was not theirs to redefine.

Even worse were the assumptions about where I came from. "What part of Mexico are you from?" some would ask, as though being Mexican was the only plausible answer. And once they found out I was Colombian, the questions turned darker. "Did you bring any cocaine with you?" one man joked. The stereotype of Pablo Escobar had overshadowed the richness of my culture.

Though I was never ashamed of my roots, those moments made me feel invisible, like my identity had been reduced to a stereotype. But instead of retreating into silence, I chose to speak louder, to educate, and to correct these misunderstandings with patience. Each time I did, I reclaimed a little more of who I was.

Finding Strength in My Heritage: A Defining Moment

It wasn't until the summer of 2009 that I truly felt a turning point in my journey. I received an unexpected invitation to speak at a Bar

Association meeting at the prestigious Ambassador Hotel in Chicago. This was not an opportunity I had sought out but one that was handed to me by Mr. H.T., a friend of my longtime friend Mike O'Malley, who had heard about my journey. He believed my story was worth sharing, and so he invited me to speak.

The presentation was short, just five minutes, but it felt like a momentous occasion. Standing in front of a room full of accomplished individuals, speaking about my journey as an immigrant striving to succeed, I felt an overwhelming sense of pride. It was a powerful moment, a reminder that despite the obstacles, I was moving forward, inching closer to my goals, and finding my place in a world that had once felt so foreign.

Embracing My Dual Identity: Beyond Nationality

As much as my Colombian roots shape me, they are not the sole definition of who I am. Over the years, I've come to realize that identity is not confined to one place, one culture, or one set of expectations. My sense of self is a dynamic tapestry woven from my heritage and my global experiences. While my roots anchor me, my branches reach out to touch the wider world.

I no longer see myself as belonging only to Colombia or America but as part of a global community. I am a citizen of the world, equally at home in the barrios of Bogotá and the upscale neighborhoods of Austin, Texas. I move between spaces with ease, carrying my heritage with pride but also embracing the richness of every place I encounter.

This broader perspective has been liberating. It has allowed me to find strength in my identity without being constrained by it. I no longer feel like I'm stuck between two worlds. Instead, I see myself as part of a larger, interconnected community where cultural diversity is not just something to be tolerated but something to be celebrated.

Today, I embrace my heritage with open arms. I find joy in educating others about Colombia—a country of vibrant culture, delicious coffee, beautiful roses, and talented people. The more I share about my background, the more I realize that embracing who I am doesn't just benefit me—it benefits everyone around me. Through my experiences, I've learned that belonging isn't about fitting into a single mold. It's about embracing who you are and allowing others the space to do the same.

My identity is fluid, complex, and ever-evolving, shaped by my past but open to the future. As I navigate my place in this world, I celebrate the beauty of cultural exchange, the strength found in diversity, and the joy of knowing that belonging is something I create, not something I have to find.

CHAPTER 9 – MOTHERHOOD

"Children are God's love gift; they are heaven's generous reward."

Psalm 127:3.

The Dream of Motherhood

The dream of starting a family had always lived within me. It wasn't just a distant wish—it was a deep, instinctual pull, like a whisper in the back of my mind that grew louder as time passed. But I knew there was something I had to do first. I had to finish my degree, stand on my own two feet, and achieve my professional goals before I could take the leap into motherhood. And then, when the moment finally came, everything else fell into place.

I met Reid, a man whose heartbeat to the same rhythm as mine. Together, we dreamt of building a family. His love for me and the strength of our shared faith made it easy to take that next step. With God's blessings, we were gifted with two beautiful children, each one a testament to the love we had nurtured between us. They are our greatest gift—a fulfillment of dreams we have built together.

The Early Struggles

The joy of pregnancy came with its own set of challenges. My first pregnancy was plagued by hyperemesis gravidarum—an illness that made it impossible to keep solid food down. My stomach churned constantly, and the relentless vomiting didn't stop. There were days when I couldn't even lift my head off the pillow without feeling like the world was spinning around me. Nine times a day, I lost the nourishment I so desperately needed. My body became frail. My spirit cracked a little each time.

Still, despite the suffering, I held onto hope. I told myself it would get better soon. Surely, this wasn't how it would be for the entire pregnancy. Then came the day of the first fetal sonogram.

I had been counting down the days to this moment—excited to see my baby, to hear the heartbeat once again. But suddenly, the fetal-maternal doctor looked like something wasn't right. His brow furrowed slightly. The warmth from the gel on my belly couldn't calm the growing unease that crept into my heart.

"They are enlarged," he said, his voice carefully neutral. "The ventricles in your baby's brain are enlarged."

My breath caught in my throat. The image on the screen began to feel less like a miracle and more like a puzzle I wasn't equipped to solve. The doctor couldn't pinpoint the cause. I was asked to come back the following week for monitoring.

The Diagnosis

The weeks passed, and the sonograms revealed more troubling news. The ventricles in my baby's brain continued to grow. "It's likely hydrocephalus," He said, the words hanging in the air like a heavyweight. The fetal-maternal doctor spoke of early delivery, of the possibility of a shunt if the condition worsened. But no one knew for certain.

I tried to push the anxiety aside, to stay hopeful. But when the day came for the birth, I had already braced myself for something I didn't understand. The uncertainty gnawed at me. As I held my breath through contractions, I clung to the thought that everything would be alright.

A Dark Diagnosis

The good news was around week 32 the ventricles simply stopped being enlarged and continue to remain stable. I was induced at 37 weeks and four days—earlier than I had planned but necessary. Less than 24 hours after delivery, a pediatrician entered my room. His steps echoed down the sterile hallway, each footfall heavier than the last.

He glanced at me with a grim expression. His words blurred together. I only caught one phrase: *"The baby is missing a part of the brain."*

I felt the room tilt beneath me as though the floor had disappeared entirely. It was as if the world had paused, and I couldn't hear or see anything but the reverberating echo of those words. Missing a part of the brain. My mind raced as the doctor spoke of the corpus callosum, also known as agenesis of the corpus callosum.

The doctors then spoke of possible developmental delays, difficulty swallowing, and learning disabilities. The possibilities they laid out were bleak, filled with words that seemed foreign and unsettling. But I wasn't ready to give up. No, I wasn't going to let that define our future or the future of our child.

Fighting for Our Child

I took a deep breath, determined. I began researching. I dug into everything I could find about early childhood development. I found early education programs that focused on stimulating the brain and growth. I spoke with experts, seeking every bit of knowledge that could help my son thrive. Every word I read seemed to reinforce what I knew in my gut: this wasn't the end. This was just the beginning.

I enrolled him in an early education program. I met with the director, sharing my hopes and my fears, asking for the utmost care and support for him. His diagnosis may have been a setback, but I refused to see it as a sentence.

A New Beginning

As my son grew, we continued to see progress. The signs were subtle at first. His motor skills were somewhat delayed, but not enough to hold him back. We enrolled him in Taekwondo. At first, he struggled to keep up with the other kids, his movements clumsy and uncertain. But slowly, he began to catch up. His confidence bloomed. I saw him find joy in the martial arts, his spirit lifting as he mastered new moves. He was thriving, and that was proof of what early intervention, faith, and sheer determination could achieve. But the journey wasn't easy. It had taken us five years to even consider having another child.

The Return of Hyperemesis

In 2020, just as the world grappled with the COVID-19 pandemic, we planned our second pregnancy. I'd hoped this pregnancy would be easier, but my hyperemesis gravidarum returned with a vengeance. Around week 11, I had to be hospitalized to control the constant vomiting. The weight of it was unbearable. I would sit on the edge of my hospital bed, staring out the window, wondering why anyone would willingly go through this.

But I knew why. I knew what awaited on the other side. A family. A child. And that was worth every moment of suffering.

A Dangerous Accident

At 28 weeks of pregnancy, just as I was starting my first job as a nurse practitioner making house calls, I experienced a terrifying accident. I was visiting an elderly couple in San Angelo, Texas when the chair I was sitting on gave way beneath me. I crashed to the floor, my head slamming into the brick fireplace. Blood poured from the wound, and I managed to call 911 before everything became a blur.

I didn't lose consciousness, but the experience shook me to my core. As I pressed a hand to my bleeding head, I knew how much I had to lose. The baby. My body. Everything I had worked for. Thankfully, I was able to go home after treatment, but I couldn't shake the fear. A part of me, a deep, primal part, feared the worst.

Health Crisis and Pre-Eclampsia

By week 32, I could barely move from my bed to the chair. The exhaustion weighed on me, my body protesting every movement. I felt weaker each day, and that's when I knew something wasn't right. I asked Reid to take me to the hospital. Tests confirmed I was in a pre-eclamptic state. The doctors told me I needed to be hospitalized immediately.

The stress of it all culminated in another emergency. At week 34, I was induced once again. My body had failed me—my pregnancy had become too risky to continue.

The Separation

We arranged for a friend to watch our son while we were at the hospital, but eventually, my sister-in-law flew in from Chicago to take him with her. As I lay in the sterile hospital bed, still groggy from medications, I felt the sting of separation. The world outside was continuing, but I was in limbo. Our baby girl was born, but my body felt foreign and unresponsive. The magnesium drips made my mind foggy, and the hospital was so overcrowded that I was placed in a tiny room that felt more like a closet than a place of healing.

My daughter was struggling to maintain her oxygen levels, and as my heart ached for her, I had to stay behind in Round Rock as she was rushed to the NICU in Austin. He went back and forth between Round Rock and Austin. He was torn because he wanted to be with me, but our little girl needed him as well. The isolation I felt was suffocating. My older son was thousands of miles away in Chicago, my husband was with our daughter, and I was left in that small room, drifting between delirium and longing.

Five agonizing days later, I was finally well enough to visit my daughter. She was ready to come home, a small but mighty miracle. The journey to recovery was long, but it was a journey I would take, fueled by the love for the family I could finally be with again.

The Winter Storm

Just as we started to settle into life with our newborn daughter, another challenge emerged. A massive winter storm hit, and we were trapped in our house with no electricity, no water, and no phone service. The temperature inside dropped to 60 degrees. We knew we had to leave. I managed to find an old phone with a different carrier and called a friend who lived across town.

What should have been a short eight-minute drive turned into an hour-long journey through the snow. We spent the next five days huddled at her home with four other families and our premature daughter. The experience left its mark on all of us, but we made it through.

The trauma of the separation and the uncertainty during that time stayed with our son. His teacher called to express concern about his behavior. Whenever it rained, he would cry, staring out the window. "My mom and dad aren't coming," he would say. The storm, the hospital, the pandemic—all of it had taken a toll on him.

Resilience and Growth

This chapter of our lives was filled with challenges, but through it all, we faced them together. We grew as individuals, as a couple, and as a family. Each obstacle, each moment of despair, only served to strengthen our resolve. We discovered the incredible power of resilience and the unshakable bond of love that held us together.

CHAPTER 10 – FIGHT, FIGHT, FIGHT...

"When you are wronged repeatedly, the worst thing you can do is continue taking it--fight back!"

— Donald Trump

The Journey of Success

Success is not a destination—it's a relentless journey. The feeling of standing on the precipice of failure, looking at what seems like an insurmountable wall, only to take one more step forward despite the weight of doubt—that's what success feels like. It's not a single moment of triumph but the thousand small battles where you choose to continue fighting. It's a tapestry woven with ambition, resilience, and an unwavering commitment to growth.

Success doesn't simply arrive on a silver platter; it is forged in discomfort, in moments when the odds seem insurmountable, and in the act of stepping into the unknown. It is the courage to push beyond familiar boundaries, to risk failure, and to learn from each mistake along the way. It is what fuels resilience, inspires growth, and motivates us to continue moving forward, even when the road ahead is rocky. And that courage? It resides within us all, waiting to be nurtured and ignited.

A Fire Within: The Power of Determination

Within me burns a fire that ignites every time someone tells me, "No." One incident stick out—a time when I had to face rejection head-on. A mentor, with the best of intentions, told me it was "impractical" to continue pursuing my dream of becoming a physician in Colombia, given my financial struggles. But I refused to accept that. At that moment, I didn't just feel the heat of my ambition; I felt the weight of every "no" that had come before.

It wasn't about being stubborn, though I admit stubbornness played its part. It was about something deeper, refusing to let others define my limitations or box me into their view of what was possible. It was a decision to transform rejection into fuel for my fire. And that fire has powered every success since, whether big or small. Every "no" is a call to action, a challenge to push harder, aim higher, and refuse to be confined by others' doubts.

Overcoming Barriers: A Journey to Becoming a Nurse Practitioner

One defining chapter of my journey was securing preceptors for my clinical nurse practitioner training. This wasn't just an academic hurdle—it felt like a personal betrayal by the world. For years, I had been told that the path I had chosen wasn't enough, that nursing was a fallback for those who couldn't cut it in medicine. But I knew differently. My dream of becoming a physician may have seemed impossible, but nursing was never a compromise—it was a calling.

I remember a moment when I thought I might not make it. It was late one night when I received yet another rejection. My phone felt heavier in my hand. The world outside seemed to mock me with its indifference. But I couldn't stop there. I thought back to that day when I had been told "No" and how my refusal to be boxed in had driven me this far. I reached out to more contacts, attended more networking events, and eventually found mentors who believed in my potential. Without those people, I wouldn't be where I am today, but I determined that kept me moving forward.

A Question That Stung: Proving My Worth

A few years prior, at my graduation party after earning my BSN in nursing, someone asked, "You're so smart. Why didn't you go to medical school?" I could feel the undercurrent of doubt in that question. There was an assumption that nursing was a "lesser" option, a backup plan for those who couldn't make it in medicine. But the question made me reflect on my path. Nursing wasn't my second choice; it was the path I had chosen deliberately, one rooted in a deep desire to make a tangible impact on people's lives.

At that moment, I didn't just defend my decision to pursue nursing; I reaffirmed my passion for the profession. I knew that nursing required just as much intelligence, compassion, and skill as any other medical field. It wasn't about "settling" for less—it was about answering a calling.

Fighting the Doubts: The Immigrant Experience

As an immigrant from Colombia with English as my second language, every day felt like a battle. Every misunderstanding, every awkward interaction, every misstep in the workplace added another layer of doubt. Yet, there was no room for hesitation. I could have let those doubts define me. I could have retreated, letting the weight of my background hold me back. But I refused.

One day, as I navigated my new role as a provider, a patient questioned my role, asking again, "Where is the doctor?" At first, I was frustrated. But instead of retreating, I stood my ground. I explained, once again, that I was the one responsible for her care. Slowly, over the course of the visit, I could see her trust building. By the end of the appointment, she nodded, her trust earned not by my title but by my actions.

These moments were challenging, but they also reaffirmed my belief in the power of determination. I have never had the luxury of letting others' doubts—about my background, my abilities, or my dreams—hold me back. Every misstep, every challenge, has become a stepping stone. With relentless optimism, I set goals and pursue them with everything I have, no matter how daunting the odds.

The True Measure of Success

Life is unpredictable, and obstacles are inevitable. But the journey doesn't end when things go wrong. Even if I don't reach every goal, I know that effort and perseverance matter more than any single success. Too often, the people who fail are the ones who never even try. I've always been determined to be the one who tries, the one who fights, the one who pushes through—no matter what.

Success is not about perfection. It's not about an unbroken string of victories. It's about having the strength to rise after every fall, the courage to keep going despite the unknowns, and the belief that even setbacks are simply steps forward in disguise. Success is defined by the willingness to keep fighting, to keep moving forward, and to make the most of every moment.

We all have the power to light that fire within. We all can pursue our passions with unwavering determination. And that, I believe, is what success truly is.

Chapter 11 – Weathering the Storm

"The struggle of life is one of our greatest blessings. It makes us patient, sensitive, and Godlike. It teaches us that although the world is full of suffering, it is also full of the overcoming of it.

— Helen Keller

The Struggle as a Blessing

Would you believe me if I told you I've faced bullying more than once in my life? The first time, I was in seventh grade. I can still picture it: the hot sun casting shadows on the balcony, the faint chatter of children playing below. I had no idea what was coming. One moment, I was simply walking with my classmates, and the next, a girl pushed me. The world tilted as I felt the cool metal of the railing against my back. I scrambled to keep my balance, my heart pounding in my chest, as I glanced down, terrified at the drop below. My breath hitched in my throat as I clung to the balcony, feeling like the earth itself wanted to swallow me whole.

In that instant, my mind raced—what was happening? Why was she doing this? The fear tightened in my chest, and I was sure I would fall. Then, like a flash of lightning, I felt her hands slip away from me. I didn't fall, but I knew I had been closer to disaster than I'd ever realized. I was shaken but not defeated.

My mom, without hesitation, transferred me to a new school. She didn't ask questions or wait to see if things would improve. Her protective instinct took over. It wasn't just about getting me away from danger; it was about saving me from something deeper—the emotional damage of becoming just another statistic. I still admire her for that. She didn't just keep me safe physically; she shielded me from the darker effects of bullying, from the scars it could leave on my spirit.

Workplace Bullies

Fast forward to many years later, and I found myself facing a similar situation in the workplace. It wasn't on a balcony this time, but the feeling of being singled out, targeted, and belittled remained the same. I was working as a receptionist in a bustling office when a colleague—a woman around my age—seemed to take pleasure in belittling me. At first, it was subtle, almost imperceptible: the cutting remarks disguised as "jokes," the looks that said more than words ever could. But it didn't take long for the tension to rise. Every time I spoke up in meetings, she would dismiss my ideas with a roll of her eyes or a snide comment.

One day, during a team meeting, I suggested a small change to our office procedure. Her eyes narrowed, and with a smirk, she immediately shot down my idea, making a sarcastic remark that echoed through the room. I felt my face flush with embarrassment, my mind scrambling to formulate a response, but I kept quiet. Inside, I wanted to scream, but I chose not to let her words define me.

I refused to let her negativity control me. I worked harder, proving my value not just through words but through actions. And while I kept moving forward in my career, she seemed to be stuck, perpetually unhappy. That taught me resilience—how to keep my head high in the face of someone who tried to bring me down.

The Fear of Losing Myself

Standing against injustice has always been a crucial part of my journey. But there was one fear that lingered—the fear of losing my sense of fairness while defending myself. Anger has never been my go-to response. Instead, I often chose silence. It wasn't because I was weak or afraid—it was because I didn't want to cross into rage. I didn't want to become someone I couldn't recognize.

But silence, I learned, was a powerful tool. It wasn't a weakness, though others might interpret it that way. I wasn't giving up or submitting. No, I was holding myself in check. I took a step back, choosing to process rather than react. Some people saw this as an invitation to walk all over me, but it was the opposite. I was waiting, watching, understanding. I believed, deep down, that good would prevail, even if it took time.

Once, at a job, I was told I was "too much." I had been labeled an overachiever, someone who worked too hard, someone who made the others look bad. I can still hear the dismissive tone: "Maybe you should tone it down a little. It's not about who works the hardest; it's about fitting in." I was baffled. Wasn't work ethic something to be proud of? But in the world I was in, it seemed that standing out wasn't always a good thing.

Learning Generosity Without Exploitation

That experience taught me a valuable lesson: balance is crucial, especially in professional environments. For example, I often found myself cleaning the stress lab machines during my breaks. It wasn't because anyone asked me to, but because I wanted to contribute. But I quickly realized that not everyone saw it as a simple act of kindness. They saw it as me trying to outshine them, a desperate attempt to prove myself.

It wasn't about the machines—it was about creating a positive atmosphere. But I also learned an important lesson in generosity: it's possible to give without letting others take advantage of you. Sometimes, kindness is misunderstood, and people mistake it for weakness. But kindness isn't a flaw; it's a strength.

Cultural Adaptation and the Struggle to Fit In

Adapting to a new culture and society was one of the most difficult transitions of my life. I felt like an outsider navigating a world where my honesty and openness were met with suspicion. In my culture, being direct and truthful wasn't just normal—it was expected. But in this new environment, my straightforwardness was often seen as blunt or overly aggressive.

I remember a conversation with a colleague. I asked her for her opinion on a project, but the way I phrased it—direct and to the point—seemed to throw her off. Her face stiffened, and she glanced away. It made me question myself. Was I wrong to be so upfront?

It became clear to me that my style of communication, though honest, was often perceived as cold and sometimes even rude. I became known as the "New Yorker" of the office, even though I wasn't from New York. It was a constant reminder of how different my cultural background was from what others were accustomed to.

But over time, I learned to adjust my approach. I softened my directness without compromising who I was. It wasn't about fitting in—it was about finding balance staying true to myself while respecting the nuances of a new culture. That was a struggle, but it was one I was willing to fight.

Bringing Energy to the Room

I've never been one to shy away from crowds. I enjoy stepping up and bringing energy to a gathering, especially when the atmosphere feels flat. I've walked into rooms where the vibe is supposed to be celebratory, yet it feels more like a corporate meeting. In those moments, one question always pops into my head: Where's the music?

The answer is simple—give me a speaker, a microphone, and Wi-Fi, and I'll turn the room around. One time, at a dull dinner party, I spotted a small Bluetooth speaker sitting unused in the corner. Without hesitation, I plugged it in, hit play, and suddenly, the room was filled with the upbeat rhythm of an old favorite. I grabbed the microphone and, before anyone could protest, started an impromptu karaoke session.

At first, people hesitated. But little by little, laughter filled the air, and one by one, my colleagues joined in. Before long, what had started as a stiff, awkward gathering turned into a night of fun, music, and shared joy. It wasn't just about singing—it was about creating an atmosphere where everyone could let loose, forget about the tension, and embrace the moment.

Facing Jealousy and Criticism

Do you think I've faced jealousy for bringing that energy? Absolutely. There's always someone who isn't happy with your enthusiasm, someone who feels threatened by the new person taking charge. I've felt the side glances, heard the muttered comments—"Who does she think she is?" or "Isn't she the new girl?" It's the unspoken judgment that stings, but I've learned not to let it deter me.

When I see an opportunity to lead or create something meaningful, I take it. And yes, sometimes it ruffles feathers. I feel the negative energy, the discomfort from those who wish they could step up but hold back. But I won't apologize for being who I am.

Some people appreciate my efforts. They see the positive impact, the way the energy shifts. Others, however, judge without understanding. They don't know my story, and they certainly don't know my motivations. But I don't need their approval. I stay true to myself as long as I'm not crossing any legal, moral, or ethical lines.

I'd rather face a bit of negativity for being authentic than hold back and wonder what could have been.

In the end, all these struggles—the bullying, the workplace challenges, the cultural adjustments—have shaped me. They've taught me the value of kindness, the importance of boundaries, and the strength of staying true to myself. And most importantly, they've shown me that life's struggles, though difficult, are often the very things that help us grow.

Chapter 12 – Beyond Survival: Thriving

"Thriving isn't just about surviving; it's about moving forward, embracing challenges, and growing from them."

— ***Unknown***

A Garden in Bloom: The Metaphor of Thriving

When I think about thriving, the first image that comes to mind is a garden. I can still picture it in the early morning light, dew collecting on the petals, the scent of fresh earth mingling with the damp leaves. Weeds creep around the edges, trying to overtake the delicate flowers, but the roses stand firm, their petals unfurling, regardless of the storm the night before. It's not a perfect garden, but it's thriving.

That's how I've come to see life—not as a pristine, unblemished picture of success, but as a messy, beautiful journey of growth and resilience. Like the garden, life is often messy. We face challenges that try to knock us down. But despite the setbacks, something in us pushes through, much like the flowers that bloom despite the storm.

The Illusion of Perfection: Mistaking Survival for Thriving

There was a time when I mistook thriving for simply checking off boxes: a stable job, a comfortable home, and a list of accomplishments. On the outside, everything looked perfect, but something felt missing. I thought thriving meant making sure my life looked flawless from the outside and that success could be measured by external markers. But life had a different lesson in store for me.

Then came the setback. It wasn't just a minor obstacle; it was a career blow that felt like a landslide, burying all the plans I had so carefully constructed. I remember sitting there, completely numb, as the reality of it hit me. At first, I felt like a failure. The world seemed to confirm it—everyone else seemed to be moving forward while I was stuck in place.

But something unexpected happened in the aftermath of that setback. Stripped of the structure I had built my life around, I began to see the cracks in my foundation. For the first time, I questioned everything—my career choices, my goals, my values. The walls I had so carefully erected crumbled, and I found myself standing in the ruins, unsure of what to do next. And that's when the realization hit me: I hadn't been thriving. I had simply been surviving.

The Road to Resilience: Embracing the Journey

Thriving isn't about ticking off a list of achievements—it's about how we respond when life doesn't go as planned. I had to take a hard look at my life and ask myself: What truly matters? What do I want to stand for? What do I want my life to represent? It wasn't an easy process. I had to confront fears and insecurities I had buried for years. The road to self-awareness wasn't smooth. But in those moments of doubt and self-reflection, I learned something crucial: resilience isn't about bouncing back to where we were before. It's about moving forward and using setbacks as stepping stones to something better.

One morning, as I sat by the window with a cup of coffee, journaling about the life I truly wanted, I felt a glimmer of hope for the first time in months. For the first time in years, I allowed myself to dream freely—without the constraints of what I thought I "should" do. I wrote about the kind of work that would excite me, the relationships

I wanted to nurture, and the passions I had long neglected. The simple act of envisioning a new path felt like the first green shoot pushing through the soil after a long winter. It was the beginning of a new season in my life, a season of growth.

Thriving is Personal: Aligning with What Matters

I came to understand that thriving is deeply personal. It's not about following someone else's script for success. It's about aligning your life with your own values and beliefs. It's about embracing your unique journey and finding meaning even in the chaos.

For me, thriving meant prioritizing self-care in ways I had never done before. It meant setting boundaries—saying no to things that drained me so I could say yes to what truly mattered. It meant reconnecting with friends and family, leaning on them during tough times, and realizing that thriving isn't a solo endeavor. It's a shared experience, one that thrives in community, love, and support.

I began to value the simple things: the feeling of waking up early for a quiet moment before the day starts, taking walks outside, and listening to the sounds of the world waking up. It wasn't about dramatic changes but about making small, meaningful adjustments to how I spent my time and energy.

Learning from Pain: Thriving Through the Storms

I also realized that thriving doesn't mean living a life free of pain or difficulty. Some of the most profound growth I've experienced came from my most challenging moments. I remember the day I received news of a personal loss. The phone call, the silence, the overwhelming grief. It hit me hard. But in that grief, something shifted. I found strength I didn't know I had. It wasn't about avoiding the storm; it was about learning to dance in the rain. It was about finding moments of peace and joy even in the midst of sorrow.

In those dark moments, I realized that thriving doesn't mean avoiding pain; it means finding meaning in the struggle and using it to grow. There is a certain kind of resilience that is born out of pain, and in the depths of my grief, I discovered a strength I could never have imagined.

A Shift in Perspective: Letting Go of Perfection

Looking back now, I can see how those challenges shaped me into someone I barely recognize—in the best way possible. I learned to let go of perfection and embrace authenticity. Thriving became less about achieving an ideal and more about progress. It's about celebrating the small victories along the way and being kind to yourself when things don't go as planned.

I now understand that thriving isn't a destination. It's a continuous process, a mindset, a practice we choose every day. There are still tough days, but I no longer measure my success by external achievements. I measure it by how I show up for myself, how I face challenges, and how I continue to evolve.

The Power of Thriving: An Invitation to Grow

As I write this chapter, I'm reminded of why I started this book. I want to share these lessons with others who might feel like they're just surviving, hoping to inspire them to embark on their own thriving journey. If I've learned one thing, it's that thriving is not a destination—it's a way of being. It's a practice that involves making choices every day to live a life that feels meaningful, authentic, and aligned with who you truly are.

So, here's to thriving, embracing the messiness of life, growing through challenges, and creating a life that feels rich, meaningful, and uniquely yours. It's not about the accolades or the external markers of success. It's about who we become along the way—the person who chooses to grow, to flourish, and to embrace the journey, no matter where it leads.

A Challenge for You:

Take a moment to reflect: What areas of your life are you simply surviving in? What would it look like to thrive in those spaces? Thriving is not about waiting for the perfect moment. It's about stepping into the messiness of life and choosing to grow, no matter the circumstances. So, as you move forward, I encourage you to embrace your own journey of thriving, no matter how imperfect or challenging it may be. You are capable of more than simply enduring—you are capable of flourishing.

Chapter 13 – Lessons on Resilience

"You may have to fight a battle more than once to win it."

— Margaret Thatcher

In the unpredictable journey of life, resilience is the greatest teacher. Margaret Thatcher's words, *"You may have to fight a battle more than once to win it,"* perfectly capture the essence of my story. Each challenge, setback, and period of personal growth has shaped me into who I am today. But at the heart of it all, there has been one constant: faith.

The Early Lessons

I grew up watching my father kneel beside his chair, the Bible resting open on his lap. His steady, familiar voice would fill the room as he recited stories of Jesus, teaching me how to pray with unwavering conviction. There was something sacred in those moments—something that whispered to my heart that even when life feels like it is breaking apart, there is always something to hold on to.

"Setbacks are inevitable, but they are not permanent," my father would say. "Trust God's plan, and you will stand firm."

I took those words with me, even when my own setbacks began to pile up. I've faced my share of battles, the kind that shakes you to your core. There were times when failure left me wondering if I would ever be enough. But I learned that resilience is not about avoiding hardship—it's about how we respond to it. In the depths of my struggle, I found my strength in the small moments when I chose to keep going.

The Weight of Doubt

There was one night when I was wrestling with doubt. A failed project lingered in my mind, and as I sat in my car parked outside my home, the weight of defeat threatened to crush me. The late summer air felt heavy, the sound of crickets a soft reminder that time continued to move forward, whether I was ready or not.

I stared at the dashboard; my fingers wrapped around the steering wheel. My breath came in shallow bursts, my mind racing with everything I had done wrong.

At that moment, I heard my father's voice, not from the past, but as if he were sitting next to me: *"This is not the end. You're stronger than you think. Trust in the plan."*

It wasn't an immediate fix, but I felt a shift. A quiet peace, like a soft breeze moving through the window, began to settle in. I wasn't alone in this struggle. There was still a purpose to the pain.

Faith as a Lifeline

Faith didn't make the pain go away, but it helped me endure it. I remember kneeling by my bed during my darkest days. Tears blurred my vision, and my voice cracked as I poured out my fears and frustrations. Each prayer became a release as if I were slowly letting go of the burdens I had been carrying alone. For the first time, I felt like I wasn't standing at the edge of an abyss. There was a sense of relief, as though God had reached out and touched my soul.

In those moments, scripture became my guide. I would open my Bible and let the words soak in like a balm for a wounded heart. Stories of resilience from Job, David, and Paul inspired me. Their challenges mirrored my own, yet they persevered through faith.

I thought of Job, sitting in the ashes, the weight of his suffering unbearable. Yet, he never abandoned his faith. His story became a constant reminder to me that suffering is not without purpose. It shapes us, refines us, and, ultimately, brings us closer to understanding God's greater plan.

The Gift of Community

Faith didn't just come from within. In Alabama, during one of the most challenging periods of my life, I found a church community that became my rock. I had been attending for a few months when a woman named Mary approached me after service. Her eyes were filled with kindness, and she offered a simple yet powerful statement: *"I will pray for you."*

I didn't know how much I needed that until I felt the warmth of her words settle into my heart. The families I met at that church became my extended family. We shared prayers, laughter, and tears, reminding each other of the strength that comes from community. Their support was like an anchor when I felt myself drifting in a storm.

The words from Galatians 6:2— *"Bear one another's burdens, and so fulfill the law of Christ."*—took on new meaning. I began to understand that resilience is not just about standing alone but about allowing others to walk with us, share our burdens, and help us heal.

Letting Go of Emotional Baggage

Another crucial part of resilience is forgiveness. There was a time when I carried bitterness toward others and even myself. Each grudge felt like a weight on my heart, preventing me from moving forward. But in prayer, I learned to release those emotions, letting go of anger and resentment.

One evening, as I sat in the quiet of my living room, I reflected on the verse from Ephesians 4:31-32: *"Get rid of all bitterness, rage and anger, brawling and slander, along with every form of malice. Be kind and compassionate to one another, forgiving each other, just as in Christ God forgave you."* The words felt like a challenge but also a liberation. I whispered a prayer, asking for the strength to forgive not only others but myself as well.

With each act of forgiveness, I felt lighter. The weight of past mistakes slowly lifted, allowing me to move forward with a heart open to new possibilities.

Finding Lightness in Struggle

One of the most important lessons I've learned is that resilience also requires us to find light amidst the heaviness of life. Humor has been a lifeline for me—when the weight of the world felt too heavy, I learned to laugh at my mistakes to find joy in the simple moments.

I remember one afternoon, frustrated by yet another setback, I walked into the kitchen to make tea. I fumbled with the kettle, spilling water all over the counter. Instead of cursing my luck, I started laughing. The absurdity of the situation lightened my mood, reminding me that life is too short to take seriously all the time. That moment of laughter, fleeting as it was, gave me the energy to face the next challenge.

Mindfulness and Reflection

In my journey, mindfulness has been key. It was easy to react impulsively, to let emotions take the wheel. But, I learned to pause, breathe, and reflect before responding. Whether in moments of stress or joy, I began to take a step back and assess my emotions, choosing how to respond with intention rather than impulse.

This practice brought clarity. It helped me stay grounded in times of chaos and reminded me that I don't always have to control everything. Sometimes, the best thing I can do is simply breathe and trust that things will unfold as they are meant to.

Surrendering to God's Strength

As the apostle Paul wrote in 2 Corinthians 12:9, *"My grace is sufficient for you, for my power is made perfect in weakness."* Over time, I've come to understand that resilience isn't about doing it all alone. It's about surrendering to God's strength and accepting my limitations. In moments of weakness, I found the greatest strength of all—the peace that comes from knowing I am not carrying life's burdens by myself.

Resilience Through Faith

Resilience is not something we can acquire overnight. It's a skill we build, moment by moment, through faith, community, and an unwavering belief that we are never alone. Every setback has been a lesson, every doubt an opportunity to deepen my faith, and every victory—no matter how small—a reminder of God's strength within me.

Margaret Thatcher's words ring true: *"You may have to fight a battle more than once to win it."* But with each battle, I have grown stronger. Life's challenges are not meant to break us but to shape us, deepen our faith, and teach us to lean on the One who holds it all.

Conclusion: Embracing the Journey

Today, when I face difficulties, I no longer see them as roadblocks. I see them as stepping stones, opportunities to grow, trust, and progress. Faith doesn't eliminate the struggles—it gives them purpose. And that purpose has carried me through, shaping me into the resilient, hopeful, and deeply rooted person I am today.

Chapter 14 – Overcoming Fear

"I learned that courage was not the absence of fear but the triumph over it. The brave man is not he who does not feel afraid, but he who conquers that fear."

– Nelson Mandela

The Instinctual Grip of Fear

Fear is an instinctual response, a primal force embedded in our biology to protect us. It warns us of danger, sharpens our senses, and prepares us for action. But fear, when left unchecked, can also hold us back. It can keep us confined within the walls of our own limitations.

I remember the first time fear truly gripped me, paralyzing me with doubt. I was preparing to speak in front of a large audience, and my stomach twisted into knots. My hands were clammy, my heart raced. I felt a rush of doubt, a voice in my head telling me to back down. But then, a thought whispered through the noise: "I may be afraid, but here I am."

At that moment, fear felt larger than life, a looming shadow threatening to swallow me whole. But I refused to let it. Instead, I took a step forward, reciting my mantra in my head. The fear didn't vanish, but I chose not to be consumed by it. I decided to face it, and in doing so, I shrank that overwhelming shadow into something much smaller.

Fear is often like that—larger in our minds than it is. It's an illusion, a shadow that looms large when we avoid confronting it. Yet when we take action, when we choose to face it head-on, the shadow shrinks. It reveals itself for what it truly is: an obstacle to overcome, not a reason to retreat.

The Mantra: "I May Be Afraid, But Here I Am"

Over time, I've learned to use a simple phrase as my anchor in times of fear. "I may be afraid, but here I am." It's not about being fearless. Fear is a part of who I am, as it is for all of us. But what matters is how I respond to that fear. This mantra became my compass, guiding me through moments of doubt and uncertainty.

One of the most significant moments I remember was during a pivotal decision at work. I had been offered a leadership role that came with its own set of challenges and fears. The fear of failure, the fear of not being good enough—it all crept in. I stood at my desk, staring at the offer letter, and the doubt tried to take hold. But instead of running from it, I repeated my mantra, "I may be afraid, but here I am." The fear didn't disappear, but in that moment, I found the strength to accept the challenge.

That phrase became more than just words—it became my tool for confronting fear, acknowledging it, and moving forward despite it.

Facing the Shadow: How Fear Shrinks When Confronted

Fear, like a shadow, often grows the more we avoid it. The more we run from it, the larger it becomes. But when we face it directly, something remarkable happens it diminishes. The tension I once felt in situations that terrified me—speaking publicly, confronting someone difficult—slowly started to lessen.

I remember standing up to a bully at school, a moment that changed the way I saw fear. I could hear my heart pounding in my chest as I walked toward him, but I didn't stop. My legs felt heavy as if the fear would keep me rooted to the spot, but I forced myself to move. When I finally confronted him, I was shocked by how small the situation seemed at the moment. The fear I'd carried with me for so long—of confrontation, of standing up for myself—dissipated once I faced it directly.

The fear had seemed enormous before, but it was nothing more than a fleeting emotion, a shadow that evaporated when exposed to the light of action. The lesson I learned from that moment is simple: fear shrinks when we step toward it, not away from it.

Courage in the Face of Adversity

Growing up in a volatile environment, fear was something I became intimately familiar with. I spent much of my childhood afraid—afraid of the violence that marked my home, afraid for the safety of my mother, and afraid of the unknown. But in that environment, I didn't have the luxury of letting fear control me. It wasn't about being fearless; it was about survival.

I vividly recall a night when I was about 10 years old. My father was angry, and the tension in the house was unbearable. I could hear my mother's soft voice trying to calm him, but I knew it wouldn't work. My fear for her safety rose like a tidal wave. But at that moment, something shifted in me. I didn't run or hide. I stood between them, my small frame shaking but my voice steady. I told him to stop. I told him it was wrong.

That night, I realized that fear was not something to escape but something to challenge. In that moment, I chose to confront the fear of harm, to protect the person I loved. It wasn't an act of defiance—it was an act of courage born from the necessity of the situation. That experience taught me that courage isn't the absence of fear; it's the ability to act despite it.

The Relentless Spirit: "If I Have to Go Down, I Will Go Down Fighting"

The mantra I adopted early on, "If I have to go down, I will go down fighting," isn't about seeking danger or conflict—it's about standing firm in the face of adversity. In times of uncertainty, when fear grips tightly, this mantra becomes my rallying cry. It's a reminder that I don't give up easily.

This spirit was forged in the crucible of my childhood when survival was the only option. It's the driving force behind my decisions, my resilience, and my willingness to face whatever challenges come my way. Fear may try to push me down, but I stand up and fight. Not with violence, but with resolve, with the determination to move forward despite the fear.

Fear as a Catalyst for Growth

Fear is a constant companion, but it doesn't have to define us. It can be the catalyst for growth, pushing us to expand our limits to face what we once thought was impossible. I've learned to see fear as an opportunity, a moment to grow. Instead of running away, I lean into the discomfort, knowing that growth lies just beyond it.

One of the most significant growth experiences came when I started my own business. The fear of failure, the fear of not succeeding—it was overwhelming. I questioned myself constantly: What if I wasn't good enough? What if it all fell apart? But instead of retreating, I chose to confront those fears head-on. I took action, even when it felt like the odds were stacked against me. And in doing so, I realized that fear wasn't my enemy; it was my guide, pushing me to become more than I ever thought possible.

Fear can be a powerful motivator, compelling us to move beyond our comfort zones. It forces us to confront our limitations and unlock our potential. It's only when we face fear directly that we truly discover what we're capable of.

Choosing to Confront Fear

Fear is just a feeling. What matters is how we respond to it. Do we let it paralyze us, or do we use it to propel ourselves forward? The choice is ours.

I've made my choice: I will confront fear, not avoid it. I will stand tall in its presence and refuse to let it control my life. Fear will always be there, lurking in the corners of our minds, but it doesn't have to be the driver of our actions. We have the power to choose how we respond to it.

In the end, it's not the absence of fear that defines us; it's our ability to act despite it. Fear may always linger, but by facing it head-on, we take away its power. We take control of our destinies and choose the life we want to live.

CHAPTER 15 – THE POWER OF EXPRESSION AND INDIVIDUALITY

"Your time is limited, so don't waste it living someone else's life. Don't be trapped by dogma – which is living with the results of other people's thinking."

– Steve Jobs

The Drive to Be Heard

From the moment I could speak, there was a force inside me pushing to be heard. It wasn't just about talking; it was about sharing my thoughts, my experiences, my very essence. I recall sitting at the dinner table, words tumbling out faster than I could organize them. My parents, listening intently, sometimes exchanged glances, eyebrows raised as I continued, a torrent of words spilling from me. But in those moments, I didn't need their approval. I felt seen. I felt understood. Communication wasn't just a skill; it was my connection to the world.

I didn't stop at words. I gestured wildly, my hands painting pictures in the air, my face lighting up with every thought. When I was excited, my eyes sparkled, telling their own story. These weren't just expressions; they were extensions of my voice. The more I spoke, the more I felt how deeply communication could shape lives. It wasn't just about relaying information; it was about creating bridges, about seeing and being seen.

The Thrill of Intellectual Discovery

In school, I gravitated toward debate clubs and literary discussions. I remember my first debate, standing before a room of students, the adrenaline pumping through my veins as I argued passionately about a current event. It wasn't about winning or losing; it was about the rush of ideas flying back and forth, the mental stretch, the back-and-forth that made me question my own beliefs. I was learning not just to defend my views but to challenge them to listen to opposing arguments without immediately discarding them.

When I joined literary discussions, something else clicked. I still recall the first time I read *To Kill a Mockingbird*, the weight of the characters' struggles sitting heavily with me. I couldn't stop thinking about them, their complexity, their flaws. When I discussed it with friends, we found ourselves in heated exchanges about the nature of morality about what it meant to fight for justice. Some of us admired Atticus Finch as a beacon of integrity, while others questioned his idealism. Those conversations weren't just about literature; they were about life. About how words could mirror the full breadth of the human experience.

The Art of Listening: Embracing Silence

As I grew older, the importance of listening began to surface. I used to think communication was all about speaking, but I learned that silence could hold as much power as words. I remember one conversation with a close friend during my teenage years when I shared my excitement about a new book. I went on and on, my words spilling out, but she didn't say much. The silence grew heavy between us, and for a moment, I questioned myself. Was she bored? Was she uninterested? But later, I understood—she wasn't disengaged. She was listening. She was letting my words settle in before responding. It was in that silence that I understood listening wasn't passive—it was an act of respect. She didn't need to fill the space with words; she needed time to process, to reflect. It was an act of deep connection.

I learned to balance speaking with listening, finding strength in moments of quiet. I remember my teacher pulling me aside once, a gentle smile on her face, as she said, "You have so much to offer, but sometimes, it's important to let others have the space to speak." Those words stung a little. But they marked a shift. I wasn't just speaking for the sake of filling silence; I was learning to listen, to create space for others to share their own stories. And in that space, I found deeper connections.

Labels and Perceptions

Despite my best efforts, people still misunderstood me. I could feel it, like a constant undercurrent—being labeled, being judged before I even opened my mouth. At my first job, during a heated meeting, I tried to offer some insights, eager to contribute, but the looks I received made me feel like an outsider. One of my colleagues muttered under his breath, "You don't have to have an answer for everything." That hit me like a slap. But instead of fighting back, I paused, feeling the weight of his words. Was I coming across as a know-it-all? As someone who thought she had all the answers? I reflected and realized that my eagerness to share might have been misinterpreted. That's when I decided to shift my approach—asking more questions drawing others into the conversation rather than dominating it. Slowly, I learned that communication isn't just about proving a point; it's about creating a space where everyone's voice is heard.

The Power of Silence

With time, I also realized the power of silence. I used to believe that confidence meant always having something to say, but now I understand that silence can speak volumes. I learned this from my mother, a woman of few words. During a difficult period of my life, she didn't offer advice. She didn't try to fix things with words. Instead, she simply sat with me. Her presence, quiet and steady, was a form of support I hadn't fully appreciated until later. In that silence, I realized that sometimes, just being there for someone is enough.

Breaking Free from Labels

When I first moved to the U.S., I felt the weight of labels like a stone tied around my neck. I wasn't seen as an individual; I was reduced to the label of "Hispanic immigrant." People didn't ask me who I was—they asked me where I was from as if that could define me entirely. I still remember a stranger's comment the first time I told them I was Hispanic. With a grin, they said, "Oh, you must love tacos." The words were innocent enough, but they left me feeling small as if a stereotype could sum up my entire identity. It made me wonder: Was that all they saw? Was that all I was allowed to be?

The label stuck. It was as though everyone expected me to fit a mold, to play a role others had written for me. In a literature class, when I shared my thoughts on a book, my professor remarked, "You're so articulate for someone from your background." Her words, though unintentional, carried the weight of assumptions. They were meant to compliment, but they revealed a subtle judgment. I wasn't just articulate for someone of my ethnicity; I was articulate, period. At that moment, I understood—those labels weren't just external pressures. They were the chains I had to break to be seen for who I truly was.

Embracing Individuality in a Diverse World

But as much as I fought against the labels, I also felt the pull of community. There was a comfort in belonging to a group that shared my background and my culture. At family gatherings, I would listen to stories passed down through generations, a sense of shared history filling the air. Yet, as much as I loved these moments, I began to feel a quiet dissonance. I wanted to contribute something different, something uniquely mine. Not just a reflection of our collective experience, but a piece of who I was—who I had yet to discover.

It wasn't easy to step outside those expectations, to pursue dreams others didn't immediately associate with someone like me. I remember walking into my first corporate meeting, surrounded by seasoned professionals. My heart raced, but I stood tall, my voice steady, my ideas clear. I wasn't there just as a minority—I was there as someone with something to offer. And when I spoke up, I could feel the room shift. My colleagues, at first surprised, eventually saw me not just as a representative of my background but as a person with thoughts and insights that mattered.

The Challenge of Color Blindness

As I continued to embrace my individuality, I also grappled with societal initiatives like Diversity, Equity, and Inclusion (DEI). While I saw the importance of addressing inequalities, I realized that sometimes, these efforts risked reinforcing the very labels they sought to dissolve. At a corporate panel, I was introduced not as a professional with insights but as "the Hispanic representative." I was grateful for the acknowledgment, but it felt like I was being reduced to a label again. I wasn't just a Hispanic woman; I was a person who had earned her place at the table.

The Gift of Individuality

Reflecting on this journey, I am reminded of Ralph Waldo Emerson's words: *"The greatest accomplishment is being yourself in a world constantly trying to make you something else."* Embracing individuality isn't just a personal victory; it's an act of defiance. It's a refusal to let the world fit us into boxes. By reclaiming my individuality, I've not only found my truest self but have also been able to contribute something uniquely mine. And in doing so, I hope to inspire others to do the same—to live authentically and to see the richness in every unique, valuable individual.

Chapter 16 – The Anchor of Faith

"Now faith is the assurance of things hoped for, the conviction of things not seen."

— Hebrews 11:1

Ronald Reagan once said: "The American Dream is not about government handouts; it's about opportunity. It's about a country where everyone has the chance to achieve their own success through hard work and determination."

His words echo deeply in my life. For me, the American Dream has never been about waiting for help but about seizing opportunities and working relentlessly to carve out a future on my own terms. Reagan's vision emphasized hard work, perseverance, and personal responsibility—not dependence on external aid. This philosophy aligns with my beliefs and mirrors the lessons I learned from my mother. Her strength, integrity, and unwavering faith have been my guiding lights, continually inspiring me to live a life rooted in these same principles.

On the morning of December 12, 1999, I stood at a crossroads. This day wasn't just about a calendar date—it marked the moment when my commitment to honoring my mother's legacy became a lifelong mission. This mission was about more than personal achievement; it was about living a life that embodied the values she instilled in me—honesty, faith, and justice. I remembered her quiet strength and how her actions demonstrated the power of resilience and character. Success, as she taught me, was not measured by accolades or wealth but by the integrity of one's character and the positive impact we had on others.

That December day solidified the realization that life wouldn't hand me success. I had to work for it. When I started college, I was the first in my family to attend, and the weight of my mother's expectations was both a gift and a challenge. I wasn't sure where my path would lead, but I knew I had to keep moving forward. My first job as a receptionist was filled with uncertainty. I fumbled through tasks with little experience and often felt out of place, but my mother's lessons echoed in my mind: showing up was half the battle. Even when it felt like walking into the unknown, I showed up every day, determined to do the work. Whether it was answering phones or navigating office life, each challenge became a stepping stone toward something greater.

Believing again is not passive hope—it is an active renewal of faith. It's about rising and trying again, even when everything feels uncertain. The road has not always been smooth, and I've faced moments where giving up seemed easier than pushing forward. But in those moments, faith became essential. I've fallen many times and questioned if I was on the right path, but each fall taught me an important lesson: growth happens when we rise again.

The act of getting up again goes beyond physical endurance. It's about emotional and spiritual resilience. It's about finding hope in the darkest moments and summoning the courage to heal and move forward. There was a time during my early career when everything felt overwhelming. I was facing challenges at work and struggling with difficult relationships. One night, exhausted and on the verge of a breakdown, I whispered a prayer for guidance. It wasn't a grand revelation but a quiet resolve. Though I didn't know the future, I knew I wasn't alone in my journey, and that was enough to help me find strength.

Life is like a canvas. We are artists, and every choice and moment contributes to the painting of our lives. The brushstrokes may not always be graceful, and sometimes we must erase and redo parts of our lives, but it's all part of the process. I've made choices that led to unexpected results, and not all of them were perfect. Some jobs didn't work out, relationships ended, and opportunities I missed. But these experiences added depth and texture to my life, shaping who I am today and giving my story meaning.

Renewing my faith doesn't mean ignoring life's difficulties. It means embracing those challenges with gratitude and determination. Each step—forward or backward—contributes to growth and self-discovery. I've had to dig deep to keep going, but in those moments, I remembered my mother's lessons: never give up, always hold onto my integrity, and trust in the process. There was a moment when I thought I might fail, but that was also the moment I realized I was closer to success than I had ever been. It was in those moments of vulnerability that I found my strength.

In the end, life is shaped by our choices and resilience. Believing again is a declaration of agency, an acknowledgment that while we cannot control everything, we can control how we respond, how we interpret events, and how we grow. Looking back, I realize my story reflects not just my dreams but my unshakable faith in the power of perseverance. Every setback, failure, and challenge has strengthened my resolve. My life stands as a testament to the transformative power of faith, perseverance, and the relentless pursuit of a dream.

Even in the face of hardship, we have the strength to create a life of meaning. We honor the legacies of those who came before us and contribute to a brighter future. Through it all, I've learned that believing again is not just about recovery; it's about rebirth. It's about finding the courage to rise, time and time again.

My Christian faith is the foundation of who I am, shaping every decision, interaction, and thought. It's not about rituals, traditions, or organized religion—it's about a deeply personal relationship with Jesus Christ. This connection transcends boundaries; it's not about following rules but about walking alongside Him, aligning my life with His teachings.

Each day, I wake up with the quiet awareness that I am not alone. In moments of doubt or challenge, I feel His presence guiding me through life. This relationship provides comfort, purpose, and reassurance. I am reminded that I am loved beyond measure, and this knowledge sustains me through life's ups and downs.

Jesus' sacrifice on the cross is central to my faith—the ultimate act of love offering salvation to all who believe. For me, this truth anchors my life. Through His sacrifice, I am forgiven, redeemed, and given the promise of eternal life. This isn't just hope for the future; it changes how I live today. His love is a light that guides me through the darkness, helping me navigate life's complexities. Knowing that I am loved by a Savior who gave everything for me gives me the strength to persevere and the wisdom to live with purpose.

Everyday, I strive to live in a way that reflects my faith. It's not about perfection but about constant growth. One morning, sitting in a coffee shop, I overheard a conversation between two strangers. One was struggling with a difficult decision, unsure of the right path. Without thinking, I leaned over and offered a few words of encouragement. At that moment, I felt Jesus' love guiding me to be a light in someone's darkness. Faith isn't just about what happens after we die; it's about how we live now. It shapes how I view the world and interact with people, guiding every action and decision.

A profound aspect of my faith is the belief in the sanctity of life. Every life, no matter how small, has intrinsic value because God creates it. I hold the conviction that from the moment of conception, life is sacred. I've witnessed firsthand the challenges surrounding life decisions. I recall a woman I met at a pregnancy care center considering abortion. Her heart was heavy with uncertainty, but I saw in her the potential of life. I offered her support, reminding her that no matter the choice, there was always hope, grace, and a way forward.

Being a conservative is not just a political stance for me; it reflects my commitment to integrity, honesty, and decency. These principles guide my actions, shaping the person I strive to be. True success isn't measured by wealth or power but by the impact we have on others and the integrity with which we live. In moments when I've been tempted to take shortcuts, I've remembered that success built on lies is never real success. The real measure is how I treat others and live out my faith, especially when no one is watching.

My faith is not just something I carry with me in crises—it's a daily journey that shapes my decisions, interactions, and worldview. Even when life's challenges seem overwhelming, I find peace knowing that I am not walking this path alone. Each day is an opportunity to live out my faith, make a positive difference, and honor God in all I do. This is who I am and the path I choose to walk, guided by the love and wisdom of my Savior.

Chapter 17 – Love, The Ultimate Sacrifice

"If I speak in the tongues[a] of men or angels, but do not have love, I am only a resounding gong or a clanging cymbal. 2 If I have the gift of prophecy and can fathom all mysteries and all knowledge, and if I have a faith that can move mountains, but do not have love, I am nothing. 3 If I give all I possess to the poor and give over my body to hardship that I may boast,[b] but do not have love, I gain nothing."

— Corinthians 13: 1-4

The True Power of Love

Love is a quiet force that doesn't demand recognition or applause. It reveals itself not in grand gestures but in the small, selfless moments that pass unnoticed by many. The true power of love isn't in how we feel but in what we do for others, often without them even asking.

I remember a night when I was deeply sick, barely able to keep my eyes open, yet my mother stayed up beside me, her hand resting gently on my forehead, wiping away the sweat from my brow. She didn't say a word—her silence spoke volumes, louder than any comforting words could. Her presence was enough, and in that stillness, I felt the depth of her love. She was not only there physically, but her love enveloped me, providing solace and safety.

At that moment, I understood what love really is. It's a steady hand in the darkness, a constant presence in the storm. It isn't loud or boastful—it simply *is*. It's a quiet comfort, a sacrifice made without thought of recognition, a gesture of love that carries no expectation.

Love Tested: A Journey Through Darkness

There came a time when love truly tested me when it stretched me beyond what I thought I could endure. Someone close to me was battling a deep depression, weighed down by their own invisible burdens. Their pain was so heavy it seemed to swallow everything around them. And yet, they didn't ask for help. They didn't demand anything from me.

But I couldn't turn away. So, I showed up, day after day, when it was inconvenient, when I was tired, when I felt as though I had nothing left to give. There were nights when I sat beside them in silence, my own heart heavy with their grief. Sometimes, I didn't know what to say, but I knew my presence was enough. I held their hand when they couldn't speak. I stayed up late to keep them company when they felt alone in their darkness.

I learned that love isn't about having the right words or solutions. It's about being there when everything else seems to fall apart when the world feels too heavy to bear. It's the quiet strength of showing up, even when the road is uncertain. Love demands that we give of ourselves, even when we feel empty.

The Pain of Forgiveness

Forgiveness was never easy for me. Anger hurt, and disappointment had woven themselves into the fabric of my past, and letting go seemed impossible at times. There were moments when the weight of the past felt unbearable when the people who hurt me seemed beyond redemption, and I wondered if I could ever truly forgive them. But love, once again, whispered to me: *Let go. Be patient. Try again.*

So, I did. I forgave. Slowly, painfully, I allowed myself to release the anger that had consumed me. Each time I forgave, I felt a piece of myself healing—like peeling back the layers of bitterness and discovering the gentleness underneath. Forgiveness stretched me, refined me, and taught me that love is not about forgetting the wrongs done to us but about choosing peace over pain compassion over resentment.

It wasn't always easy. It wasn't always immediate. But with each act of forgiveness, I grew stronger. Love challenged me, refined me, and made me better, pushing me toward a place of empathy and understanding I didn't know I could reach.

Love's Transformative Force

Looking back on my life, I can see how love has been the driving force behind my most significant achievements—achievements that didn't come from seeking recognition but from the desire to give something meaningful to others. Love gave me the courage to take risks, to step out of my comfort zone, and to chase dreams that once seemed impossible.

Without love, my actions would have felt hollow. Relationships would have been shallow, lacking the depth and connection that love fosters. It is love that has given my life purpose and meaning. Love is the thread that weaves together the fabric of my humanity, guides me when the path ahead is unclear, and gives me the strength to keep going when the world feels uncertain.

But love is not merely human. There is a divine love that transcends our earthly understanding, a love that calls us to be more than just ourselves. When I think of the phrase "God is love," I am reminded of the purest form of love—unconditional, boundless, and self-giving.

Experiencing Divine Love in the Everyday

I feel this divine love not in grand displays but in the everyday moments that reveal something greater than myself. I see it when a stranger offers a kind word to someone who is struggling. I see it in the quiet forgiveness shared between friends. I see it in the love that passes between a mother and child, unspoken yet deeply understood.

These moments are glimpses of a love that is infinite and beyond comprehension. It's a love that calls us to be better, to give without expectation, to serve without asking for anything in return. I've seen this love in my own life—in the grace I've received when I've faltered, in the forgiveness I've offered when it seemed impossible, and in the kindness of others when I needed it most.

Love, in its purest form, isn't just an emotion we feel. It is something we live every day, through every action, every decision. It is the divine love that sustains us, that connects us to one another and to something greater than ourselves.

The Foundation of Our Lives

Love connects us to one another, to our communities, and to the divine. It transforms us from individuals into a collective, reminding us that we are all part of something greater than ourselves. Love is the force that compels us to create, nurture, forgive, and grow. It is the story we are all a part of, the story that binds us together and gives our lives meaning.

When I think about love now, I no longer see it as just an emotion or a fleeting feeling. I see it as the foundation upon which we build everything—the relationships we cherish, the communities we create, the faith that sustains us. Love is the ultimate sacrifice because it asks us to give of ourselves freely, without reserve, and without expectation.

And for that, I am endlessly grateful. For love, in all its forms, has made me who I am today and will continue to shape who I become tomorrow.

Chapter 18 – A New Beginning: The Family We Built

"Family is not an important thing. It's everything."

— Michael J. Fox

A Quiet Morning in Our Home

The sun has barely risen, casting a soft glow across the kitchen counter as I watch my children, still in their pajamas, laugh with their father. Reid is stirring his coffee, his quiet smile a constant source of warmth. Our son, with his wild hair, is jumping around the living room, making up a silly dance, while our daughter watches, giggling uncontrollably. It's the kind of morning I once thought was a distant dream.

In contrast, I remember waking up as a child to the sound of raised voices, the smell of cold coffee, and tension thick in the air. Mornings were unpredictable. Sometimes, they were filled with the weight of an argument that lingered throughout the day; other times, they were silent, as though we were all walking on eggshells, hoping to avoid triggering another outburst. The thought of a peaceful morning, filled with laughter and simple joys, felt as impossible as wishing for sunshine on the darkest days.

But today, as I sit back and watch my family interact, I realize how far I've come. This moment of calm, this unity in the midst of our everyday routine, is the fruit of hard work, faith, and love. It's a reality I never imagined in the shadows of my past, but here it is, unfolding before me, each day more beautiful than the last.

The Stability We've Built

I look over at Reid, his steady presence a grounding force in our home. There's a simplicity to his actions that brings peace—like when he's helping our son with his homework, patiently explaining a math problem for the third time. I watch how our daughter leans into his side, trusting that he will always be there to support her. I can feel the warmth between them, the way they rely on each other, and I realize that this bond we share—this stability—is something I never had growing up.

I think back to my childhood, to the years spent in a house that never felt like home. I remember the times I would hide in my room, listening to the sound of my parents arguing in the kitchen, unsure of who was in the right but certain that love had somehow been lost in the shuffle of broken promises. There was no reassurance, no knowing glance from a partner that said, "We're in this together." The uncertainty in my house was palpable. The silence was loud and deafening because no one was brave enough to speak what we all knew was true—things weren't okay.

But now, in this home, I see something different. I see Reid as a man who is not afraid to talk about feelings, not afraid to show affection, and not afraid to lead with kindness. I feel his support in every action, from the way he helps me with the kids to the way he holds my hand when I need comfort. His love for our family is unwavering, and it creates the foundation for everything we do together.

Parenting with Love, Not Fear

As I watch our children grow, I'm struck by how different their childhood is from mine. They are free to express themselves, to voice their opinions, and to ask questions without fear of judgment or reprimand. I hear our son tell a joke that makes his sister laugh uncontrollably, and I smile, thinking of the laughter that fills our home each day. I had never heard such unfiltered joy in my childhood. The laughter I remember was often forced as if we were all pretending to be okay when nothing truly was.

I remember a specific moment when I realized just how different their lives are from mine. One afternoon, our son came to me asking if she could invite one of his friends over for to play. It was a small request, but what struck me was her certainty that he could ask without feeling like he was imposing or that her request would be dismissed. He knew that her voice mattered. He knew that her feelings were valued.

I think back to when I was his age. I was often around family members who were too busy to even acknowledge my presence. I was rarely given the chance to just be a child, to have my voice heard, and yet here my son and daughter are both comfortable in their own skin, with their needs met with love.

This is what I fought for—the right to give my children the kind of childhood I never had: one filled with acceptance, understanding, and an unwavering belief that they deserve to be heard and loved for who they are.

Forgiveness and Healing: A Lifelong Journey

Healing from the wounds of my past was not instantaneous. It took time, effort, and more courage than I ever thought I had. It meant coming face-to-face with the pain of growing up in a house where love was conditional, where I was never quite sure of my place. There were nights when I cried alone, wishing I could undo the years of turmoil, wishing I could feel the safety and security I so desperately needed as a child.

But through faith, therapy, and the unconditional love of my husband, I found my way back to myself. I found peace in knowing that I could forgive—both those who had hurt me and myself for allowing the past to define my future. I had to learn to let go of the chains of resentment that had held me hostage for so long. Forgiveness didn't come easily, and it didn't come without struggle, but it came, and with it, healing.

I remember a moment when I realized I had forgiven—truly forgiven—my parents for their failed relationship. I was sitting in my car, reflecting on the path I had walked to get here when the thought struck me. I wasn't angry anymore. I had let go of the bitterness that once consumed me. In its place was a quiet understanding that they, too, had their own struggles, their own demons they couldn't face. And with that realization, I felt a weight lift off my chest. I wasn't bound to my past anymore. I had the freedom to choose who I was to build a future that was rooted in love, not pain.

A Legacy of Love and Faith

What I treasure most now is the legacy I am building with my family. It's not about wealth, success, or accolades. It's about the values we pass down, the love we share, and the faith that sustains us. When I look at my children, I see a future full of hope, possibility, and love. I see them growing up in a home where they are cherished, where they are taught to love themselves, to love others, and to honor their faith.

I think of the legacy I was handed—a legacy of dysfunction, of silence, of fear—and I am grateful that I was able to break that cycle.

I gave my children a legacy of love, trust, and faith. I gave them the courage to succeed, not just in the traditional sense of achievements and accolades but in the deeper understanding of living a life filled with purpose, meaning, and love.

As I watch my children laugh, as I feel Reid's hand in mine, as I reflect on the home we've built together, I know that this is what success looks like. It's not about overcoming the odds for the sake of accolades. It's about creating something lasting—a family, a home, a life—that reflects all the best parts of who I am, who we are, and who we strive to be every day.

This is the legacy I am proud to leave—a true American dream, built not on the foundation of wealth or status but on love, faith, and the courage to break free from the past and create a future that is ours to shape.

Made in the USA
Columbia, SC
14 June 2025

4529bf51-f326-4066-8852-00d8662b5b0eR02